"In *The Instructional Leader in YOU*, Danny Steele has hit the home run that all principals have needed for years. This book was written for me and other leaders who have a desire to lead and learn better so we can empower others. The powerful relationships and curiosity that are formed in a school culture that prioritizes instruction and learning are the cornerstones of this book. It is filled with real-life examples and research-based evidence that will help any leader improve. I will read this one twice, for sure."

Salome Thomas-EL, EdD, *Award-Winning Principal and Author*

"In *The Instructional Leader in YOU*, Danny Steele masterfully combines relatable anecdotes, practical strategies, and genuine insights that empower leaders at every stage of their journey. This book isn't filled with abstract theories; it's packed with real-world, actionable steps to help you become the instructional leader your teachers and students deserve. If you're ready to lead with intention, purpose, and heart, this is the book you need on your desk!"

Thomas C. Murray, *Best-Selling Author, Director of Innovation, Future Ready Schools*

"Danny Steele gets it. *The Instructional Leader in YOU* speaks to the real work of school leaders—the kind that doesn't always show up in a job description. With practical strategies and honest reflection, Steele reminds us that being an instructional leader isn't about knowing everything—it's about being present, being curious, and leading with purpose. This book cuts through the noise and helps principals focus on what matters most: supporting teachers, building trust, and creating a culture where learning thrives. This is the kind of leadership book that doesn't just inspire—it equips. It's one I'll return to again and again."

Emily Paschall, *Learner, Teacher, Leader, Author of Eyes on Culture: Multiply Excellence in Your School*

"Danny writes a bold and practical blueprint that redefines what it means to lead schools in today's dynamic educational landscape. With compelling insights and actionable strategies, this book empowers leaders at all levels to cultivate authentic relationships, foster professional growth, and build the collective efficacy needed to transform learning communities."

Dr. Adam Dovico, *Professor, Former Principal, Author*

"If you're a school leader who's ever felt overwhelmed by the buzz-word that is 'instructional leadership'—this book is your reset button. *The Instructional Leader in YOU* doesn't try to impress you with jargon or a 300-point walkthrough rubric. It meets you right where you are—in the hallway, in the classroom, in the chaos.

Danny Steele strips it down to what really matters: being present, being curious, being real. He reminds us that you don't need to have all the answers to lead—you just need the heart to ask the right questions and the courage to show up for your people.

This book is a high-five to every principal trying to do the work AND still be the lead learner in the building. It's practical. It's personal. It's real. And more than anything—it's a reminder that leadership is about people first, always. Read it. Share it. Live it."

Glen Hill, *Superintendent*

"What resonated with me most about this book is how intentionally Danny connected with practicing principals from across the country, along with well-known educational thought leaders, to shape each chapter. He masterfully uncovered commonalities that can support any school leader. That level of authenticity is evident in every strategy shared. This isn't just another leadership book—it's a reflective, practical resource for school leaders who want to grow in meaningful ways. Each chapter offers actionable insights grounded in real-world experience, making it both relatable and inspiring."

Ed Cosentino, *Principal*

"Reading *The Instructional Leader in YOU* was like being given user-friendly instructions for leading schools—without having to sort through a labyrinth of confusing and dense data and information. The ten strategies for every school leader are research based, clearly stated, visionary, current, and extremely helpful.

I love this book! Reading it felt like sitting down with an old friend to talk about the things we believe about leading schools and what we can do to make a difference. It was so interesting to read that it was hard to put down, and I wanted to meet every principal the author interviewed. I actually thought about which of the ten strategies I thought were my strengths in my career as a leader.

If this book had been available when I taught graduate classes in educational leadership, it would have been required reading. If it had been available when I was in a statewide leadership position, I would have sent a copy to every principal in the state. And finally, if I were starting over in my educational leadership career, this is the book I would carry with me everywhere and, more importantly, on which I consistently would try to base my actions."

Ruth Ash, *Retired Principal, Superintendent, and Dean of Education*

"As a building principal, I know firsthand how overwhelming the daily demands of school leadership can feel. In *The Instructional Leader in YOU*, Danny Steele offers a practical and refreshing guide for leaders who want to stay grounded in what matters most—supporting teachers and fostering a culture of learning. With humility, honesty, and real-world insight, he reminds us that you don't have to be an expert in everything to make a lasting impact. This book is both encouraging and actionable—an essential read for every school leader striving to grow, connect, and lead with purpose."

Zac Bauermaster, *Principal, Speaker, and Author of* Leading with a Humble Heart *and* Leading with People

"*The Instructional Leader in YOU* is a refreshing and powerful resource for school leaders who are ready to lead with both head and heart. So many books on instructional leadership feel distant—heavy on theory and light on reality. But Danny Steele offers something different. This book feels like sitting down with a trusted mentor who's walked the walk and still remembers what it's like to be in your shoes. Steele weaves together timeless leadership truths with the voices of real-world practitioners—principals who are making a difference every day. The result is a book that is wise, practical, and deeply human. With stories from the field, actionable strategies, and reflective insight, *The Instructional Leader in YOU* is the kind of book you'll come back to again and again. It's not just a read—it's a resource for growing your leadership from the inside out."

Dr. David Geurin, *Director of Greenwood Laboratory School at Missouri State University, Author of* Future Driven: Will Your Students Thrive in an Unpredictable World

"Danny has captured the essence of what it means to be an instructional leader at any level of education. The topics resonated with me as I could think back to my 20 plus years as a school level administrator. The topics are separate yet intertwined and really show the various ways that a strong instructional leader leads a school. Those who read

Danny's words with an eye on self-improvement will certainly find quality nuggets that will guide their improvement. As Danny states, 'Instructional leadership is not something you do to your faculty: it is a way of leading that makes a positive difference for your teachers and your students.' I wholeheartedly recommend this book to continue to guide your journey as an educational leader."

Jay Posick, *Semi-Retired Principal*

"*The Instructional Leader in YOU* speaks to the heart of leadership in schools. Every chapter—from curiosity to culture—reminds us that leading a school isn't about having all the answers, it's about asking the right questions, showing up with purpose, building real relationships, and empowering others. As a principal, I saw myself in these pages. If you lead people, especially in education, this book is a must-read."

Annette Sanchez, *Principal*

"In *The Instructional Leader in YOU*, Danny Steele shares experiences and practical ways for school leaders to improve and focus on things that are important, but perhaps more than anything, he offers hope and inspiration. His positive writing style as well as his authentic experiences make this book an incredible resource for principals at all types of schools and experience levels."

Dr. Robert Thornell, *Author and Former Principal*

"*The Instructional Leader in YOU* is a must-read if you are looking to accelerate your leadership potential and grow your understanding of what it really takes to be a successful school leader today. The innovative strategies and inspirational stories will provide you with the tools to reimagine your own leadership potential!"

Alonzo Barkley, *Principal*

"*The Instructional Leader in YOU* is exactly what school leaders need right now—timely, practical, and deeply grounded in real-world experience. Dr. Danny Steele has an unmatched ability to take what often gets lost in the daily whirlwind of leadership and bring it into sharp focus. This book challenges us to rethink what it means to lead instructionally, pairing clear strategies with compelling stories that resonate with leaders at every level. As someone who coaches and supports early-career principals, this is a resource I'll be putting into their hands right away."

Dr. Darrin Peppard, *Leadership Coach, Author of* Road to Awesome *and* Culture First Classrooms, *Host of the* Leaning Into Leadership *Podcast*

"A must-read for school leaders! Danny's book reminded me of what so many of us feel but rarely say out loud: that despite our best intentions, the weight of the job can often leave us feeling inadequate or overwhelmed. But Danny's words are a powerful reminder that instructional leadership is not about perfection—it's about connection. It's about walking alongside teachers, being present in classrooms, and making intentional decisions that support learning.

If you're a principal who's ever felt like you're not 'instructional enough,' this book is for you. It will encourage you, equip you, and remind you that your ability to lead instructionally comes from your ability to build trust, ask good questions, and stay relentlessly focused on student learning.

This book won't just sit on your shelf—it will live on your desk. Read it, revisit it, and most of all, share it with your leadership team."

Dr. Jennifer Hogan, *Principal*

"The Instructional Leader in YOU is the real deal! Whether you are a first year instructional leader or a veteran instructional leader, this book has something for you. Danny displays his passion and love for supporting school leaders by providing a resource that can change the instructional leadership landscape. This is a must read!"

Gregory Moore, *2024 Alabama Principal of the Year*

The Instructional Leader in You

As a principal, you wear many hats, including that of instructional leader. But it's impossible to be an expert in all areas of instruction, assessment, curriculum, and data analysis. Danny Steele takes the pressure off your shoulders and shows how you can add value to the instructional program of your school and be viewed as an instructional leader by your staff.

Steele presents ten simple strategies that can help you on your journey as you work to balance the imperatives of building operations and instruction. He shows how each strategy plays out during the school day, and he offers real-life examples and inspiration from practitioners in the field. No matter your level of experience, you'll find simple ideas that you can implement immediately.

You may feel unprepared to be an instructional leader, or you may feel too busy managing the school. But with this jargon-free, easy-to-use guide, you'll be able to embrace your role as the instructional leader of your school, so that your teachers, and more importantly your students, can benefit!

Danny Steele (@steelethoughts) worked in education for 31 years and has written six books. In 2016, he was named Alabama's Secondary Principal of the Year. He has presented at numerous state and national conferences and continues to speak at school districts around the country.

Also Available from Routledge Eye On Education
www.routledge.com/k-12

The Total Teacher: Understanding the Three Dimensions that Define Effective Educators
Danny Steele

365 Quotes for School Leaders: Inspiration and Motivation for Every Day of the Year
Danny Steele

365 Quotes for Teachers: Inspiration and Motivation for Every Day of the Year
Danny Steele

Essential Truths for Teachers
Danny Steele and Todd Whitaker

Essential Truths for Principals
Danny Steele and Todd Whitaker

The Instructional Leader in You

10 Strategies for Every School Leader

Danny Steele

Taylor & Francis Group

NEW YORK AND LONDON

Cover image: Getty Images

First published 2026
by Routledge
605 Third Avenue, New York, NY 10158

and by Routledge
4 Park Square, Milton Park, Abingdon, Oxon, OX14 4RN

Routledge is an imprint of the Taylor & Francis Group, an informa business

© 2026 Danny Steele

The right of Danny Steele to be identified as author of this work has been asserted in accordance with sections 77 and 78 of the Copyright, Designs and Patents Act 1988.

All rights reserved. No part of this book may be reprinted or reproduced or utilized in any form or by any electronic, mechanical, or other means, now known or hereafter invented, including photocopying and recording, or in any information storage or retrieval system, without permission in writing from the publishers.

Trademark notice: Product or corporate names may be trademarks or registered trademarks, and are used only for identification and explanation without intent to infringe.

ISBN: 978-1-032-97338-8 (hbk)
ISBN: 978-1-032-97340-1 (pbk)
ISBN: 978-1-003-59332-4 (ebk)

DOI: 10.4324/9781003593324

Typeset in Palatino
by codeMantra

This book is dedicated to all the school leaders out there who work day in and day out to support their teachers and create schools where students thrive.

Contents

Acknowledgements .... *xiv*
Meet the Author .... *xv*

    Introduction 1

1. A Foundation of Curiosity 11
2. The Powerful Role of Visibility 25
3. The Surprising Strength of Vulnerability 34
4. Leading Without Relationships Isn't Leading 45
5. Creating Opportunities for Growth 55
6. Delegating Is Winning 69
7. Being Intentional 79
8. Prioritizing Learning, Not Teaching 90
9. Removing Barriers 103
10. Focusing on the Culture 115
    Conclusion 130

Acknowledgements

When I contemplated writing this book, it never even crossed my mind to look for another editor. Lauren Davis and her team at Routledge have always been so supportive of my work and have always believed in my message. Lauren is the first and only editor I emailed about this book idea, and I remain grateful to have an editor who is such an enthusiastic cheerleader.

I am grateful for the many current and former school leaders who were involved in this project to one degree or another. Some of these folks reviewed my initial blog post, some met me for coffee and chatted about instructional leadership, some spent time with me on a zoom conversation talking about their experiences in their own school. At the risk of leaving someone out, I want to thank the following: Ruth Ash, Daniel Barrentine, Alonzon Barkley, Ashley Bowling, Jennifer Brown, Jeff Colgrove, Tracy Colley, Ed Cosentino, Adam Dovico, Amy Fast, Lance Forman, Emily Freeland, Sean Gaillard, Kim Hall, Jennifer Hogan, Reba Hudon, Chris Jackson, Karissa Lang, Carmen Maring, Shannon McCaskey, Ryan McClendon, Cas McWaters, Matt Miller, Chris Myles, Annette Sanchez, Kenny Southwick, Jon Wennstrom, Vic Wilson, Neely Woodley, Rick Wormeli, and Cristy York.

I would like to thank my former professor, Maurice Persall, for introducing me to the research of McREL and the Balanced Leadership Framework in graduate school many years ago. It's one of the things from grad school that has always stuck with me.

I'd like to thank my brother, David. He has spent countless hours on the phone with me, exchanging texts, and allowing me to bounce ideas off him. His insight, clarity of thought, and wisdom helping me to think through my ideas has been invaluable.

I'm grateful for the support of my three grown children who share my excitement when I achieve big milestones like this one! And finally, to my wife Holley… thank you for always supporting me, believing in me, encouraging me, and being in my corner!

Meet the Author

Danny Steele worked for 31 years in education as a principal, assistant principal, teacher, coach, and assistant professor of Instructional Leadership. In 2005, Steele was recognized as the "Secondary Assistant Principal of the Year" for the state of Alabama. And in 2016, he was recognized as Alabama's "Secondary Principal of the Year." He has written six books including two with Todd Whitaker, has presented at numerous state and national conferences, and has spoken in school districts around the country. Steele has an undergraduate degree in History from Covenant College; he has a Master's in History from the University of Alabama, Birmingham; he has an Educational Specialist degree in Educational Administration and an Educational Doctorate degree in Educational Leadership—both from Samford University. He is the father of three (mostly grown) children and resides with his wife in Birmingham, Alabama.

Introduction

The Dilemma

Two boys are sitting in the front office because they were caught horseplaying in the bathroom after lunch. The secretary has a concerned parent holding on line two. The yearbook vendor just showed up and only needs two minutes of your time. Mr. Johnson texts you that the copy machine is jammed for the third time this week. Ms. Griffin has to leave her class to go get her own child who is throwing up in the nurse's office, so the front office is scrambling to get the class covered. It is brought to your attention that a water bottle leaked the length of the front hallway, and the custodian is still at lunch. The spill needs to be cleaned up before someone slips. You take a breath, sit down at your desk, and realize you have 17 unopened emails. Two of the emails are from the district office. You better open those now. What you really want to do is visit some classrooms, and check in with some teachers on their planning period. If you work in buildings that were anything like mine, this scenario seems all too familiar and likely evokes some stressful memories. In his introduction to his own book on instructional leadership, Peter DeWitt (2020) describes the dilemma further:

> For one reason or another, many leaders seem to operate in perpetual crisis mode, which prevents them from entering into classrooms as often as they would like to. Their district leaders pull them out of the school several

times a week for meetings, professional development that is often geared toward sit-and-get compliance issues, or, ironically, to cover other buildings because that leader is out. Yes, leaders are called out of their building to deal with discipline issues in other buildings because that principal is out of district. And we wonder why instructional leadership seems so elusive. (3)

Linda Carrier (2017) writes: "The research is abundant and clear, effective leadership of schools is necessary for improved student achievement. Both the research and policy agenda of the last 20 years has also been clear; to be an effective school leader in the age of standards and high-stakes accountability specifically means being an instructional leader" (xi). Elmore (2000) claimed, "Instructional Leadership is the equivalent of the holy grail in educational administration" (7). Sadly many school leaders do not feel up to the challenge. As Carrier noted: "Many principals with whom I speak share a sense of inadequacy and question their personal level of competency. Not uncommonly they share feelings of hopelessness that they can become instructional leaders" (10–11).

This book is for the principal who isn't perfect, the principal who sometimes feels overwhelmed, who feels inadequate at times, the principal who cares deeply about teaching and learning but finds it difficult to get out from under the suffocating weight of administrivia. Early in my administrative career, I began hearing about the importance of principals being the instructional leader in their schools, and this concept actually figured significantly into my dissertation, written 20 years ago. There is copious amounts of research that indicates effective schools are led by strong instructional leaders, and every principal I have interacted with has the desire to provide that type of leadership to their school. Some principals feel trained and equipped to be the instructional leader, but the realities of managing a school (exemplified in the first paragraph) get in the way. Sadly many school leaders do not think they have the time or ability to tackle the challenge. It is tempting to think that once you're sitting in the big chair, you are expected to be the guru of instruction, assessment, curriculum, and data analysis. That sort of unreasonable expectation is overwhelming. It is my goal in writing this book to give school leaders hope. I share strategies that any school leader can integrate into their daily leadership. These strategies don't require specialized training, or specialized expertise. I suppose the requisite expertise could be the ability to understand and connect with the teachers in the building. Hopefully, that skill has already been recognized in you, and that's why you have ascended to the position you have now.

The Strategies

Being Curious

Albert Einstein once said: "I have no particular talent; I am merely inquisitive." This remarkable claim attests to the power we have to affect our own intellectual growth, as well as the instructional program of our school, through relentless curiosity. Ask lots of questions—of your teachers and of yourself. In this chapter you discover how this strategy builds a culture of continued growth in your school.

Being Visible

The principal sets the tone in the building. One of the ways you set the tone and communicate your priorities is through your presence. Your presence communicates that you value the activities the teachers are engaged in. Whether it's visiting classrooms or sitting with teachers during their professional development, your presence around the building carries weight, and it does not go unnoticed. In chapter, you'll learn how visibility helps with more than simply managing the school.

Being Vulnerable

Maybe you were a former PE teacher. Maybe you spent much of your career in the ranks of coaches. Maybe you were a chemistry teacher who just taught with a laser-like focus on your own discipline and you don't feel well rounded, academically speaking. That's okay! Don't pretend to have experience that you do not yet have, knowledge that you have not yet acquired, or skills that you have not yet mastered. Your staff probably already knows your background, so be candid with them about your learning curve. They will appreciate your transparency and vulnerability as you model for them a commitment to being the lead learner of the building. This chapter will reveal the various ways that vulnerability empowers you as an instructional leader.

Being Relational

There is a familiar adage about the importance of teachers building relationships with their students: *They don't care how much you know until they know how much you care.* This same concept applies to principals hoping to lead teachers. The teachers don't really care about your "expertise" until they know you are in their corner… until they understand you value them… until they feel your support. So get to know your teachers and support them at every opportunity! In this chapter, you'll read about the essential nature of relationships for instructional leaders… and I'll reveal the toughest lesson I ever learned as a school administrator.

Creating Opportunities for Growth

Effective instructional leaders are committed to helping teachers improve their practice. They do this through conversations with teachers that facilitate them being reflective about their own teaching and through creating opportunities for teachers to learn from each other. In this chapter you will see examples of what this strategy looks like in the school building.

Being Strategic with Delegation

As you get to know your teachers, you learn their strengths and weaknesses. You learn what they're really passionate about. You learn which teachers are most respected among their peers. There will be many opportunities during the year to leverage the "teacher leaders" in your school. Also look for opportunities to delegate managerial tasks. This gives you more time to engage with the instructional program. In this chapter you'll see a variety of examples of what delegation looks like for an effective instructional leader.

Being Intentional
Make no mistake about it, managing a school can bring some headaches. And it's easy to get bogged down in the administrivia of the job. You can't wait on your instructional leadership to happen accidentally; be intentional with how you go about your work. Make instruction and learning a priority and a consistent focus for all of your efforts. This chapter provides the nuts and bolts for school leaders aspiring to lead the instructional program.

Being Focused on Learning
I have heard it said that *until something is learned, nothing is taught*. This quip poignantly underscores the fundamental purpose of schools: student learning. Believe it or not, it's easy to lose sight of this truth. We can spend so much time focusing on the knowledge, skills, and practices of teachers that we actually take our eyes off the ball and forget the fact that learning is the core objective. This strategy is about leaders keeping the staff focused on the goal of student learning, and this chapter includes specific examples of how school leaders can do this on a daily basis.

Removing Barriers
Teachers do the core work of the school. If you can take something off their plate… if you can find a resource they need… if you can help them solve a problem… if you collaborate with them to navigate a dicey parent situation—all of this support to them in the classroom allows them to spend more time and energy on meeting the needs of their students. Make it a priority to provide teachers what they need to be effective and work to minimize whatever distracts from their primary responsibility… teaching their students. In this chapter readers discover the many subtle ways that this strategy enhances teacher effectiveness.

Being About the Culture
Teaching and learning does not happen in a vacuum. Teachers and students thrive when the culture of the school is strong. And fostering a strong culture is perhaps one of the most important things a principal can do. While culture building might not seem

like you're engaged in "instructional leadership," it will create an environment where teachers and students do their best work. And that's the goal. While culture is a broad topic, this chapter highlights five high leverage areas of focus for school leaders to build a culture that optimizes student learning.

The Format

Each chapter has a section entitled "What It Looks Like" which is intended to provide concrete, real-life examples of how the quality discussed in the chapter plays out during the school day. These examples are drawn from my own experiences as well as the experiences of principals I interviewed. It is my hope that this application piece underscores the relevant and practical nature of the strategies. Each chapter is also followed by a list of questions for reflection. These questions can serve as a springboard for a book study, or they can simply facilitate the reader crystallizing their own thoughts as they think through the lessons of the chapter and how the strategy applies to their own work environment. It is my hope that each chapter inspires many more questions of the reader.

The Research

This is a book for practitioners, not academics. However, it's important to mention that the strategies outlined in this book are grounded in research. The Midwest Regional Continental Research Laboratory (McREL) conducted a meta-analysis of the behaviors that principals engage in and which ones have a statistically significant impact on student achievement (Rouleau, 2021). They developed a "Balanced Leadership Framework" based on this research which identifies and clarifies these leadership behaviors. By my assessment, 18 of the 21 behaviors identified are accounted for in the ten strategies of this book.

Throughout this book, I also reference *Principals and Student Achievement: What the Research Says*. It is a 2003 report by Kathleen

Cotton that synthesized and summarized decades of research analyzing the impact of principals on student achievement. From the studies, Cotton is able to identify 26 traits that characterize effective principals—effective principals being those school leaders whose schools experienced increased levels of student achievement. Just as the 21 leadership behaviors in the Balanced Leadership Framework can be aligned with the ten strategies I outline in the following pages, they can also be found in the leadership traits revealed by Cotton.

So while this book is supported by research, it does not refer to it often, nor does it incorporate a lot of traditional jargon associated with the literature on instructional leadership. Rather it draws extensively on the experiences of the author and other distinguished principals who are doing the work… and doing it well. It is the hope that this approach allows the strategies outlined in this book to be both accessible and actionable for today's school leaders.

Three Disclaimers

First, readers should understand that these strategies are not practiced in a vacuum or in isolation, so they should not be viewed this way. These strategies complement one another, they work in harmony with one another, and readers will surely recognize that they often overlap. That's how leadership works.

Second, this book does not address the recruiting and hiring of personnel. Hiring talented and dedicated teachers is the single most important thing a principal can do to provide for the most effective instruction in the school. I get that. The skill of recruiting, screening, interviewing, and hiring effective teachers is an important subject; it's just not the focus of this book. I'm concerned here with how we lead the teachers we already have.

And finally, this is not a "how to" manual. In some ways, it is a reaction to that very notion. In the following pages, you will not find a list of things to do or a prescription for steps to follow tomorrow in order to be the quintessential instructional leader in your building. Consider for a moment this list of topics around instructional leadership:

- Educational philosophy
- Brain research
- Curriculum development
- Teacher–student relationships
- Learning styles
- Theories of leadership
- Curriculum mapping
- Theories of learning
- Differentiated instruction
- Instructional strategies
- Multiple intelligences
- Data-driven decision making
- Student engagement
- Walk-throughs and instructional rounds
- Assessment
- Adult learning
- Collective efficacy
- Leading change
- Professional learning communities
- Instructional coaching
- Levels of learning
- Equity
- Instructional rigor
- Culturally responsive teaching
- Mental health
- Trauma-informed practice
- Program evaluation
- Program implementation
- School improvement
- Lesson plans
- Learning targets
- Supervisory styles
- Classroom observation instruments

I'm overwhelmed writing this list and it isn't even exhaustive. All of these topics are important, and they are all worthy of study. But wow! That list is the reason the notion of being an instructional leader is a daunting one! I hope the strategies espoused in the following pages are not daunting, intimidating, or overwhelming. And I hope they provide a useful way for conceptualizing and prioritizing the qualities you hope to embody as a school leader.

The Inspiration

This book was born out of a leadership coaching session I had with a couple of young principals in the summer of 2024. The superintendent explained to me that these guys were green, and his goal was for me to develop their capacity as instructional leaders in their respective buildings. I spent a few hours with each of the principals on that first day. They were both quite humble, and they both acknowledged they were starting at ground zero with instructional leadership and they believed that it represented their steepest learning curve as novice principals. As I chatted with them and reviewed their survey results from the previous spring, it was clear to me that they had great relationships with teachers, and their teachers, to a very large degree, trusted them as the school leader. Morale in both schools seemed to be good. Consistent with the perceptions of the superintendent and the principals themselves, the teachers did not view their principal as the instructional leader of the building. But I came away from that first visit greatly encouraged. I thought to myself, "These guys are selling themselves short, and they don't know their true potential as instructional leaders." After all, building strong relationships with teachers and cultivating a positive school culture was 90 percent of the challenge. They had already done the "heavy lifting!" My goal was to empower them with the confidence that they could significantly enhance their skills and effectiveness as instructional leaders through being intentional with some basic commitments and leveraging some strategic qualities. The day after that first visit, I identified the ten strategies outlined in this book, and I quickly turned those early thoughts into a blog post. That blog post grew into this book. My hat is off to those two principals. I admire their humility and their enthusiasm for growing as leaders.

A Final Thought

If anything, these ten strategies represent a collection of dispositions, mindsets or commitments that characterize effective instructional leaders. They provide a foundation upon which school leaders can actually engage meaningfully and productively in those topics identified in that earlier, exhausting list. Principals who lead with these strategies create the context where educators in the building are able to confront their challenges and pursue their instructional goals in an organic and focused way. In his own book on the topic, Baruti Kafele (2025) asks the immensely practical question: "Are my teachers at an advantage *because* I am their leader?" (6). I firmly believe that school leaders who embrace the strategies in this book do indeed put their teachers at a distinct advantage. There is an old proverb that tells us, "The best time to plant a tree was 20 years ago. The second best time is now." You may feel unprepared to be an instructional leader, or you may feel so busy with managing a school that you are simply trusting your teachers to ensure quality learning is taking place. Whatever your perspective, *now* is a great time to embrace your role as the instructional leader of your school. Your teachers, and more importantly your students, will benefit from your dedication. Thank you for joining me in this journey.

References

Carrier, L. (2017). *Keeping the Leadership in Instructional Leadership: Developing Your Practice*. Routledge.

Cotton, K. (2003). *Principals and Student Achievement: What the Research Says*. ASCD.

DeWitt, P. (2020). *Instructional Leadership: Creating Practice out of Theory*. Corwin.

Elmore, R. (2000). *Building a New Structure for School Leadership*. Albert Shanker Institute.

Kafele, B. (2025). *What Is My Value Instructionally to the Teachers I Supervise?* ASCD.

Rouleau, K. (2021). *Balanced Leadership for Student Learning: A 2021 Update of McREL's Research-Based School Leadership Development Program*. McREL International.

1
A Foundation of Curiosity

You're already on the right track! You picked up this book! Curiosity does not take talent, skill, or expertise. But it does take humility. It requires us to acknowledge that we don't have all the answers, and we don't know everything. It also requires a certain level of care… or maybe dedication is a better word. We have to care about discovering the right answers, or at least the best answers. We have to be dedicated to ensuring that we are on the right track and that our school is on the right track. We have to care about growth and improvement. You are currently engaged in your own professional growth, so I feel safe assuming that you care about these things.

Curiosity is not an attribute that is typically included in discussion of leadership qualities, but I think it should be. Francesca Gino drew upon research to publish "The Business Case for Curiosity" (2018) in the *Harvard Business Review*. He makes the case that curiosity is foundational to effective organizational leadership, arguing, "When our curiosity is triggered, we think more deeply and rationally about decisions and come up with more creative solutions. In addition, curiosity allows leaders to gain more respect from their followers and inspires employees to develop more-trusting and more-collaborative relationships with colleagues." He also concludes from the research that a culture of curiosity results in specific benefits that include fewer decision-making errors, reduced group conflict, stronger communication, and improved team performance. When I spoke with the former principal and noted author, Rick Wormeli, he talked to me about the important role for curiosity in contingency planning. Asking yourself questions about potential issues or challenges that might arise as the result of a decision or program implementation allows you to refine and improve what you are about to do, or at the very least, it prepares and equips you to better respond to the challenges that result. One of my mentors and former principal, Cas McWaters, talked to me about the fact that curiosity is a commitment not to be satisfied with the status quo. "If you're satisfied with the way you've always done it, there's no need to be curious, right?" It is a pursuit of the "culture of excellence" that so many leaders give lip service to. He also told me that "We should be planning twice as much as what we're doing." The process of reflecting and asking questions before the action allows you to predict or anticipate potential barriers.

I have thought for many years about what differentiates education from every other profession. Surely there are a myriad of differences, but the one that I have been stuck on relates to innovation. Consider what the bottom line is in business and industry. You don't need to be a genius to know that it's the dollar—or financial profit. Businesses are in it to make money. If they do not adapt, if they do not evolve with the latest research in their field, if they do not innovate, they will become obsolete. They will go out of business.

Now consider the bottom line in education. If we were to try and quantify it, perhaps we would say standardized test scores. But I've never known a teacher who was fired for poor test scores. What incentive is there for teachers to innovate or evolve in their own practice? There are clearly many amazing teachers out there who are constantly evolving and innovating in their practice, but I think it is because of their own intrinsic motivation to be excellent in their role. The educational system does not require it. To further illustrate this contrast: imagine an orthopedist who practices with the same technique and the same technology that they used when they began their career 30 years ago. We can't imagine that... because it would never happen. Now imagine a teacher who teaches in much the same way that they have for the last 30 years. That scenario is uncomfortably easy to imagine.

Curiosity is about asking questions—about anything and everything that impacts your teachers and the experiences of their students. For an instructional leader in the school, curiosity might be reflected in questions like the following:

- Why do we pace the curriculum the way we do?
- What are ways that artificial intelligence might impact how our teachers teach and our students learn?
- I wonder how other schools are meeting the needs of English Learners.
- What sort of bell schedule works best for our students?
- Why does this teacher have such good results with her students?
- Are our students more likely to thrive if we figure out how to give them more breaks in the day?
- Are there things outside of the "instructional program" that impact the quality of teaching and learning?
- Are there lessons we can learn from successful businesses and industry?
- What would our alumni tell us about their experience in our school—positive and negative?
- Is there a better way?

DeWitt (2020) writes, "Many times, instructional leadership is about looking for the 'why' in each situation" (53). Like peeling back the layers of an onion, there are powerful insights to be discovered when we demonstrate relentless curiosity.

What It Looks Like

Building Your Personal Foundation

Perhaps most importantly, it's helpful for school leaders to reflect on their own core values and sense of purpose. Gupton (2010, p. 5) synthesized the work of Sergiovani and Starratt (2007), encouraging instructional leaders to develop an "educational platform" and suggest the following questions as a framework:

1) What are the purposes of education?
2) What should the major achievements of students be?
3) What is the role of schools in students' educational process?
4) What is the role of the learner in schools?
5) What is the purpose of the curriculum? Who should develop it?
6) What is my concept of an effective teacher?
7) What kind of pedagogy do I favor? Why do I favor this form of pedagogy?
8) What kind of teacher–student relationship is best to support learning?
9) What kind of climate is best for learning?
10) How do I perceive school leadership?
11) What is the principal's role in school leadership? How do I see myself in this role?
12) What roles should parents, community members, business leaders, teachers, staff, and students play in school leadership?

Reflecting on questions like these allow school leaders to refine and articulate their own philosophy of education and of leadership. When a principal is solidly grounded in their own core values and beliefs, they are in a better position to lead their school authentically. There will be times during your career when various views might change because of the evolving context in which you're leading or perhaps because of new research that supports different approaches. It is indeed, a sign of intellectual maturity to be able to change one's mind. But Gupton (2010) cautions principals to "Differentiate between your core beliefs and values and those open to change."

Building Professional Capacity

The principal, Karissa Lang, told me, "The curious piece is what drives us to be our best." And she emphasized that it is not always about seeking the big changes; it can be about constantly seeking the small changes or tweaks that can yield big results. Another principle I interviewed was quick to say, "We come in with certain expertise… but not all!" Daniel Barrentine talked to me about moving from middle school administration to high school. In addition to a totally new curriculum, he had to learn about different high stakes tests. He asked his colleagues questions about test construction, test format, and DOK levels. He spent a lot of time visiting classrooms to pick the brains of his teachers. Carmen Maring, a principal in Michigan, did not even have a teaching degree. She had been a school counselor. Imagine her learning curve in terms of being a leader of teachers. Imagine the level of vulnerability and curiosity it took to earn credibility with her faculty. Without a willingness to embrace her learning curve and dive into her new role with humility and an eagerness to learn, there was no way she would have earned credibility with her faculty as the instructional leader of the building. Another principal, Ashley Bowling, talked to me about the value of tapping into resources in your building through constant questioning. With an awareness that asking questions involved some vulnerability, she quipped, "Don't be envious; be curious." Alonzo Barkley stressed to me that curiosity is a tool that every administrator must have. "I think we all come in with certain skill sets, and that's what lands us the position as a school leader. It might be special education, safety, or athletics." He continued, "I might not know about 504, the curriculum of a certain content area, my accountability scores and how they're broken down, the power of instructional rounds, or professional learning communities." But he concluded that curiosity for him has been the biggest tool—being willing to ask for help, and being willing to learn. Kafele (2025) challenges school leaders with this question: "What sort of professional learning that helps you to become a better instructional leader are you exposing yourself to?" (91). Former principal and current superintendent, Amy Fast, reminded me of the "Dunning Kruger" effect which refers to a cognitive bias that essentially states those with limited competency *overestimate* their abilities while those with a higher competence may *underestimate* their skills. So for our purposes of understanding the emerging instructional leader, those who have the humility to demonstrate relentless curiosity will be the ones who excel in their own professional growth. The more questions they ask and the more they learn, the more motivated they will become to continue learning.

Feedback from Parents

Another principal, Jon Wenstrom, talked about the value of being curious in a parent conference. Asking genuine questions of the parent communicates a desire to learn about the student. It communicates that the parental perspective is valued. He told me: "It's more about the questions you ask than the answers you give." In their inspiring book, *The Power of Moments* (2017), Chip and Dan Heath talked about an elementary school that had been languishing for years. One of the defining characteristics of this struggling school was the lack of engagement from parents. They didn't know the teachers, and they didn't trust the teachers. The leadership decided to take the radical step of having teachers make home visits during the summer. In previous home visits, the engagement typically consisted of teachers talking to the parents about what they needed to know and do to help their child succeed. And they brought information to give the parents about the school. It was very much a one-sided engagement. And as you can imagine, these visits didn't do anything to foster trust with the parents. Under new leadership, a different approach was tried during these home visits. The teachers did not bring anything with them to the visits other than curiosity. Their goal was to ask parents about their child… and what their dream for their child was. They were there to learn from the parents, not lecture them about how to support their child's school. This type of curiosity doesn't just create new learning; it creates engagement and builds connection. The results were stunning. Over the next few years, parental engagement increased dramatically, as did student achievement.

Feedback from Teachers

Annette Sanchez talked to me about the value of surveying staff members to get feedback. She would wonder things like:

"We've been doing this for so long. Is it still effective?" It is easy to get quick answers to a broad range of questions like this through surveys. You'll recall that one of the principals who inspired this book learned from their teacher surveys that the faculty did not view them as instructional leaders. I recommend that teachers have the option of responding to surveys anonymously. Sometimes you will receive feedback that is hard to hear; but anonymous surveys are the best ways to get candid answers. Teachers will tell you in these surveys what their frustrations are, what their challenges are, and what their needs are. This provides the administrative team with data to make decisions about where they need to place more of their time and energy. But teachers will also tell you in the surveys about parts of their job they enjoy, things that are going well, and the types of support that they appreciate. This is the feedback that can give you the motivation to keep going, and it provides validation for the efforts that need to be continued.

When looking for feedback from teachers, though, definitely don't restrict yourself to surveys. As you move around the building, ask lots of questions. You'll be surprised how much valuable feedback you can receive when you put yourself in position to have informal conversations with your staff. These questions go a long way to communicating your support for your teachers and they also contribute to building the rapport that is the subject of Chapter 4.

Feedback from Students

The students in the school are why we exist. It is hard for me to imagine a more important challenge than assuring that the experiences of the students who walk through our doors are positive and meaningful. It's imperative that we commit ourselves to getting first-hand information from them about their experience in school. The principal, Shannon McCaskey, talked about the value of asking students about their experiences during walkthroughs. Through these informal and unscripted conversations, you can get a sense of what students are learning, to what extent they feel engaged, and what their perception of the class is. I remember one of my own conversations from a walkthrough that didn't go as I had anticipated:

Me: "Hey there… what are you working on?"
Student: "A worksheet"
Me: "I mean what are you learning about?"
Student: "Chapter 7."
Me: "Uh… I mean… why are you doing this work?"
Student: "Ms. Johnson told us to."

Yeah… this is not the type of feedback you're hoping for when talking with students about their learning experiences. Being an educator, you know that when talking to kids, the conversations don't all go as planned.

Another way for principals to learn about the experiences of their students is through "Principal Advisory" groups. This can be handled any number of ways, but the goal is to meet with a group of students with the goal of getting their feedback. I would typically order in some pizza and meet with students over lunch. There were times that I met with representatives of student government, and there were times that I asked teachers to nominate students for this group. This can also be a great way to make kids feel valued. You can ask the students what they're enjoying about their school experiences, what they're frustrations are, what types of school work they like or don't like.

One time, I interviewed a couple of students about their experiences in school, and then emailed the anonymous audio files to our teachers. It was eye-opening for the teachers to hear about experiences in the classroom from the perspective of students. School exists for the students, not the adults in the building. However we learn about their perspective of our students, it's crucial that we commit ourselves to being curious about how they experience school. Perhaps one of my favorite takeaways from DeWitt's book on instructional leadership was his systematic inclusion in each chapter of multiple segments of what he called "Student Voice Questions." These segments were intended to encourage school leaders to consider whatever the focus was of that particular chapter from the perspective of the student. Examples of these included the following:

- "How do you encourage student voice in the learning that takes place in your school?" (11)
- "When you think about the implementation of instructional strategies, or even things as profound as one-to-one initiatives, how are the strategies communicated to students? We know that strategies can have a big impact on teachers and leaders because of the sheer amount of time they take to implement. Do students feel that impact too?" (23)
- "Do students who major in career technical education (CTE) understand that you respect them as much as those students who major in liberal arts, math and science, or the arts?" (39)
- "What avenues can students take in your school when they feel alienated because of a fractured relationship with a teacher or when they do not feel like they have a voice in their own learning?" (54)
- "In what ways do you help marginalized students feel valued in your school? What images do they see when they enter the school? Are those images representative of all students?" (65)

The curiosity reflected in these questions represents a strong commitment to honoring the perspectives of students and significantly impacts your ability as a leader to lead an instructional program that creates the best opportunities for students to learn and thrive.

Questions About Teaching and Learning

Imagine this conversation between a new principal who used to be a PE teacher and an 8th grade Algebra teacher:

Principal: "What are you teaching this week?"
Teacher: "Slope intercept formula."

Principal:	"Do students pick up on that pretty quick, or is that a challenging unit?"
Teacher:	"Well, they often struggle but because our curriculum is jam packed, we just can't spend much time on it."
Principal:	"Have you thought about teaching it with a different strategy?"
Teacher:	"I have thought about it, but I'm a bit nervous to try something new."
Principal:	"Go for it! I'd love to hear how it goes!"

The principal could go on to ask the teacher about her plans for intervening with students who are struggling as well as her plans for assessing the students' level of mastery. This entire conversation can take place without the principal knowing anything about algebra. But his process of asking the teacher questions about her practices promotes reflection on her part, and that is one of the most valuable contributions an instructional leader can make. DeWitt (2020) put it succinctly: "being a content expert doesn't matter as much as asking teachers important questions about what students are learning in the classroom" (37).

Inspiring Curiosity in Teachers

When I was interviewing Ed Cosentino, a principal in Maryland, he kept talking about the value of a book by Warren Berger: *A More Beautiful Question: The Power of Inquiry to Spark Breakthrough Ideas* (2016). He described how it helped him to promote a level of inquiry with teachers. I bought the book, and it was a powerful read, indeed. I recommend it to all of you. The consultant Steve Barkley (2025) noted in a recent blog post, "curiosity enables educators to reimagine their practices and find innovative ways to engage learners." In his piece for the *Harvard Business Review*, Gino (2018) suggested the following strategies for building a culture of curiosity:

- ♦ Hire for curiosity
- ♦ Model inquisitiveness

- Emphasize learning goals
- Let employees explore and broaden their interests
- Reward employees for learning
- Have "Why?" "What if…?" and "How might we…?" days

Creating a culture of curiosity is an amazing goal for school leaders. We grow when we have the courage to ask tough questions to which we don't know the answers. Our teachers hone their own craft when they are willing to interrogate their own practices. And I have long believed that great teachers cultivate curiosity among their students. Curiosity is foundational for learning, and great schools are characterized in part by a culture that is a safe place to ask questions and that validates the practice.

Questions for Reflection

Are there things that we're doing in our school simply because we have always done them that way?

Are there instructional strategies or activities happening in some classrooms that should happen in more classrooms? How might we accomplish that?

Am I setting aside time in my day or in my week to brainstorm? To wonder about what might be? To wonder about what should be?

How can I be more intentional about uncovering the experiences of students in our school?

Are there steps that I could take to encourage innovation in the classroom?

Are there times when our instructional practices are inconsistent with our instructional philosophy? How do we address that?

What do I want our school to look like five years from now? Ten years from now?

What are ways that I encourage teachers to reflect on their own practice?

Why do some parents seem disengaged from the school and their child's education?

References

Barkley, S. (2025, January 4). The Role of Curiosity in Instructional Leadership and Coaching. *Steve Barkley Ponders Out Loud* [blog]. https://barkleypd.com/blog/the-role-of-curiosity-in-instructional-coaching-and-leadership

Berger, W. (2016). *A More Beautiful Question: The Power of Inquiry to Spark Breakthrough Ideas*. Bloomsbury USA.

DeWitt, P. (2020). *Instructional Leadership: Creating Practice out of Theory*. Corwin.

Gino, G. (2018, September–October). The Business Case for Curiosity. *Harvard Business Review*. https://hbr.org/2018/09/the-business-case-for-curiosity

Gupton, S. L. (2010). *The Instructional Leadership Toolbox: A Handbook for Improving Practice*. Corwin.

Heath, C., & Heath, D. (2017). *The Power of Moments: Why Certain Experiences of Extraordinary Impact*. Simon & Schuster.

Kafele, B. (2025). *What Is My Value Instructionally to the Teachers I Supervise?* ASCD.

Sergiovani, T., & Starratt, R. (2007). *Supervision: A Redefinition* (8th ed.). McGraw-Hill.

2
The Powerful Role of Visibility

Visibility is a cardinal virtue for school leaders. I think many administrators, though, think about being visible primarily as a way to manage the building and promote good public relations. Graduate school introduced me to the acronym MBWA (management by walking around). Without a doubt, walking around the building allows for more effective and responsive management. When you're out and about, you notice when there is a spill in the hallway. You notice when there is a classroom full of unsupervised kids because the sub hasn't shown up. You notice when two students' horseplay is about to evolve into a fight. Ed Cosentino even noted that his ubiquitous presence in the hallways saved time on emails. Because his teachers had so many opportunities to interact with him face to face, they didn't have to email him their questions. And he didn't have to read their emails! One could easily write pages of examples of how visibility facilitates more effective management of the school.

But I've also come to embrace a new acronym: LBWA (leadership by walking around). I am convinced that visibility around the school does more than ensure smooth operations; it strengthens the ability to lead teachers effectively. Smith and Andrews (1989) write, "The principal's presence is felt throughout the school as the keeper of the vision. The visible principal constantly displays behavior that reinforces school values" (18). And in her review of the research around principal behavior and student achievement, Cotton (2003) writes: "In high achieving schools, the principals do not spend their time cloistered in their offices, keeping company with administrivia. On the contrary, the researchers find them to be unwaveringly present and approachable in the everyday life of the school" (14).

I don't remember if someone taught me about the importance of being visible in and around the school, or if I just understood it intuitively, but I can say with certainty that it shaped how I went about my job as an assistant principal and then as a principal. At the first faculty meeting of a new school I was leading, I would say something like this: "I'm going to be in your classrooms a lot, so please don't be surprised. The visits usually won't be long, and it will always be my goal to avoid interrupting you or the flow of the lesson. My goal is never to bust anyone or catch them off their game. But I will visit your classrooms for three reasons. First, I love seeing students learning and engaging in cool activities. Second, I love seeing you all in your element, doing your thing. You all inspire me. And third, I want our students and staff to know I care about their experience in school. One of my teachers began calling me "Ninja" because he said he would look up and I had just appeared as if from nowhere. In addition to popping into classrooms, I would walk the halls at class change; I would hang out in the lunchroom; I would go to as many games, meets, matches, plays, concerts, or other extracurricular events as I could. And during halftime of the Friday night football game, I would stand on the 40 yard line to watch our band perform. I wanted the band members to see me cheering them on, but I also wanted their parents to see me. I am firmly convinced that some of those parents drew conclusions about my leadership abilities based on the fact that they saw me supporting their son or daughter during the halftime show. I remember one night when I was "on duty" for our basketball games. I was standing in one of my typically prominent positions along the wall, looking for one of my new assistant principals who was also on duty. I finally found him sitting in the crowd, blending in with the other fans. At half-time I talked to him about the importance of being "seen" at these events. I told him he needed to be as conspicuous as possible, not just for supervisory purposes, but for the PR value. My words to him immediately resonated; he simply hadn't thought about it in those terms.

What It Looks Like

It didn't surprise me that as I was interviewing principals for this book, all of them had examples of ways that they are visible in their role. Shannon McCaskey makes it a priority to be at carpool every morning. Yes, it's great PR for the parents to see her there, but Shannon talked to me about the value of making connections with students at the beginning of their day as she's able to welcome them to school. As she put it: "I can get a student out of the car if they're having a bad morning, talking to them, sitting down, finding out why, even referring them to a counselor before they hit the classroom. But if they get out of the car and they're already in a bad mood, that's going to transfer into what's going on in the classroom." Additionally, Shannon said that she makes a point to avoid using her phone while she's visiting classes (except when she uses an app to provide feedback to the teacher). She wants to be totally present while visiting the classroom, free from the distractions of her phone. There were actually times I left my phone in my office when I went to visit classrooms for that exact same reason. Jennifer Hogan talked about the importance of walking around as a way to connect with teachers to get a pulse on morale. She wants to know if her teachers are feeling positive or defeated. Of course she wants her teachers to be happy, but she also stressed that it was crucial to the mission of the school. As she pointed out, teachers' instructional and collaborative effectiveness do not exist in a vacuum; they thrive when morale is high. She leads a large suburban high school of around 3000 students, so you can imagine that visibility for her is a challenge. This is a good time to emphasize that instructional leadership, and everything that comes with that role, is a team effort of the entire administration. During class changes, all of her administrators have designated areas in the school, and they are encouraged to visit a few classrooms after the tardy bell rings as they make their way back to the office or whatever their next responsibility is calling them. This represents a strategic and intentional way of ensuring administrative visibility throughout the school during the entire day. Adam DoVico talked enthusiastically about visiting classrooms in his school. But he was no ninja! His face lit up as he talked about "jumping into classrooms and modeling a lesson" for teachers. School leaders definitely earn credibility with their teachers when they are comfortable teaching a lesson on the fly.

Ashley Bowling pops into benchmark meetings enough that as she said it, "her presence isn't scary anymore." Think about the value that comes from the leader's presence in teacher meetings.

- Your presence communicates that you value their work which increases the likelihood that the teachers will take the time seriously.
- Your presence provides a measure of accountability that the time will be focused and used wisely.
- Your presence allows you to gain a better understanding of the challenges or potential roadblocks that are confronting your teachers.
- Your presence allows you to celebrate the positive steps they are making.
- Your presence earns you credibility and gives you the opportunity to join in the discussion and engage in a meaningful way with the work of the teachers.

When I spoke to Tracy Colley, a former teacher of mine, she talked about the value of instructional leaders being approachable. That approachability is in large part a function of the relational leadership discussed in Chapter 4, but that approachability is also facilitated by your consistently visible presence throughout the building. Who is more approachable, the principal sitting in their office, or the principal you see walking down the hallway during the class change? There were multiple occasions where I popped into a classroom, and the teacher asked me if she could speak to me out in the hallway for a minute. On her designated break, that same teacher might have had to go to the bathroom, make copies, make a phone call, handle email, and grade some papers. She might not have had the wherewithal to make the trip down to my office to ask that same question. So my visibility in her room facilitated some important conversation. Sean Gaillard, a principal in North Carolina, shared with me some thoughts on the role of visibility:

> One of the most meaningful ways I've enhanced my instructional leadership is through the power of being visible. It's not just about being seen—it's about being *present*. My heart is always in the classroom, and I believe that to lead well, we must follow our core and be where the action is. Leadership doesn't live behind a desk. It lives in the heart of the school—the classroom—where teaching and learning happen every day. Visibility isn't just about supervision or monitoring. It's about showing up with intention, consistency, and authenticity. It's about being in service to our teachers and students. When we're present, we adopt the role of coach—cheering on, asking thoughtful questions, offering support, modeling what matters, and empowering growth. That's human-centered leadership. That's where culture is built, trust is formed, and instructional excellence takes root.

It is worth making specific reference here to the "Balanced Leadership Framework" I cited in the introduction (Rouleau, 2021). Of the 21 leadership behaviors that had a statistically significant positive impact on student achievement, the behavior with the highest correlation is what the authors referred to as "Situational Awareness." They describe this as the leader being "aware of the details and the undercurrents in the running of the school and uses this information to address current and potential problems" (4). Consider what that behavior entails and how it plays out day to day in a school. How does the leader become aware of the "details and undercurrents in the running of the school?" They become aware because of their ubiquitous presence around the school. When you're in the halls at class change, when you visit with teachers in their classrooms during their planning period, when you walk through the teacher's lounge, when you sit with teachers at their lunch table, when you hang out with teachers who have carpool duty, when you sit with teachers in their collaborative meetings… these are the moments when you hear the "scuttlebut," when you find out the things that teachers are caring about, things that are frustrating them, or things that are interfering with their work. But as the authors of the Balanced Leadership Framework point out, it's not enough to be visible and to listen, principals have to allow the insights gained to impact the decisions they make and how they lead.

So spend time visiting classrooms. Even if you don't have the wherewithal to provide written feedback to the teacher, your presence in the classroom communicates that you care about what students are learning, and you care about the work of the teacher. Find time to sit in meetings with teachers. Whenever possible join teachers in their own professional learning. Your presence communicates that you value the activities the teachers are engaged in. When you make it a priority to sit alongside your staff, they are more likely to make it a priority themselves. Being visible around your school is not just about raising staff morale or generating good public relations, your constant presence has a positive impact on the quality of student learning.

Questions for Reflection

What are the places in our school or community where I need to be more visible?

Are there some classrooms I pop into more than others? Why is that?

How is my presence in classrooms or professional learning communities perceived by the teachers?

Are there times that my presence can be perceived as "hovering" or "intimidating"?

Are there times I need to leave my phone in my office when I am walking the hallways and visiting classrooms?

Can students predict where I will be during class changes? Is that a good thing or a bad thing?

What is it that prevents me from being as visible as I would like to be and how can I mitigate those barriers?

Does the staff think that I am visible?

Does my administrative team share my value of being visible? How can I add more value to my "visibility"?

References

Cotton, K. (2003). *Principals and Student Achievement: What the Research Says*. ASCD.

Rouleau, K. (2021). *Balanced Leadership for Student Learning: A 2021 Update of McREL's Research-Based School Leadership Development Program*. McREL International.

Smith, W. F., & Andrews, R. L. (1989). *Instructional Leadership: How Principals Make a Difference*. ASCD.

3

The Surprising Strength of Vulnerability

Vulnerability is not always a quality that one associates with leadership. Leaders are strong, bold, and confident, and it's tempting to associate vulnerability with weakness, timidity, and insecurity. Although it could be considered a paradox, I think this quality is an important one for leaders, and one that allows principals to have a bigger impact on the teachers they wish to lead. Most principals would assume that instructional leadership includes topics like curriculum development, pedagogy, data analysis, research, and instructional feedback. And I am certain that 100 percent of school leaders would say these are important and worthy of their time. While the day-to-day demands of managing a school building provides a partial explanation for the lack of time that principals spend engaging with these activities, it's also likely the case that many principals also lack the confidence to wade into those waters. Curriculum and instruction is not part of the wheelhouse of many school leaders and it is likely not in their comfort zone. Cawelti (1993) suggested these tasks are often avoided "simply because principals are not comfortable with them" (x). I suggest to you that embracing one's own insecurities represents a strong path forward. This takes vulnerability, so it takes courage, but accepting the insecurity is the first step in moving past it. Karissa Lang referred to insecurity as the "Achilles heel" for many leaders. It is the lack of confidence that becomes the obstacle preventing them from addressing things that really need attention.

I first heard about the "Johari Window" sitting in Dr. Loucrecia Collins' graduate class in 2001. I was working on my administrative certification and I'm fairly certain our textbook was the one I have cited in this book, *Supervision and Instructional Leadership*, albeit an earlier edition. Dr. Collins explained that the Johari Window represented the various facets of how we are perceived. In one windowpane is how we see ourselves. In another windowpane is how others view us. In a third windowpane is our perception of how others see us. Glickman, Gordon, and Ross-Gordon (2010) label the fourth pane as the "unknown self" (16). It encompasses those aspects of ourselves of which neither we nor others are aware. Being self-aware is certainly an important interpersonal skill, but it is also incumbent upon school leaders to be aware of the potential gap that exists between the second and third panes. Ideally, the way that we believe others view us is in complete alignment with how they *actually* view us. That's not always the case though, as was true with me in a situation that was simultaneously tragic and comical. (I talk about it in Chapter 4.) It takes courage and vulnerability to acknowledge that gap. It requires a willingness to confront the fact that the positive view you have of yourself is not matched by others in the building. If you view yourself as a collaborative leader, it can be devastating to learn that others think you make decisions in isolation or that the views of the faculty are not considered. DeWitt (2020) notes there is often a disconnect between perceptions as it relates to instructional leadership, "My research shows that many principals believe they are instructional leaders, but many teachers don't share that view" (3). Glickman et al. (2010) provide further evidence on the relevance of the Johari Window to instructional leadership:

> What does the Johari Window have to do with supervision? … We may, at our discretion, decide to keep parts

> of ourselves private. (For example, we may not want teachers to know all the details of our life and personality.) We need to understand that by remaining largely private and not sharing the experiences that bind us as humans, we are creating a distance when we work with teachers. We may prefer formality and distance and may be able to document that such privateness accomplishes certain results. On the other hand, we must also accept that our privateness will be reciprocal and that staff may not easily discuss personal situations that may affect teaching performance. First, we must be aware of how private or public we are with our staff and determine if we desire teachers to be the same way with us. Second, as supervisors, we cannot afford to be blind to our own behaviors and the effect of those behaviors on others. We can improve only what we know; to believe only our own self-perceptions is to court disaster. (117)

I taught history for eight years before I began my administrative career in 2001. I didn't have a lot of experience engaging with teachers of other subjects, at least not in an academic context. As I grew into my leadership roles, I realized that if I wanted to lead teachers, I needed to enter their "world." I needed to understand what they cared about as well as their unique challenges in teaching their discipline. What follows are obviously broad generalizations, and there are always exceptions… but here are a few insights I picked up from other disciplines and grade levels. I learned that a lot of math teachers don't like to write. And there is no consensus among math teachers about the use of calculators. I learned that most science teachers love the concept of hands-on learning and having students conduct labs, but lab space is not always available. And labs take a lot of time to set up and clean up. I learned that most English teachers have favorite poems, short stories, and novels that they like to teach. I learned that the English curriculum has much less structure than other subjects, and this is a reason that it can be hard to get English teachers "on the same page." I gained an appreciation for how long it takes to grade student essays. I learned how much paperwork special education teachers had to complete and how many meetings they had to attend. I learned how passionate they are about advocating for the kids on their caseload. I learned that Career Tech teachers are masters at making their curriculum relevant to their students.

While all of my career was at the secondary level (grades 6–12), I also picked up on a few insights about elementary school teachers. They are wizards at developing structures and routines in their classrooms. They are particularly sensitive to skill development, and they demonstrate a remarkable commitment to teaching the "whole child." Additionally, I developed an appreciation for the fact that it typically takes elementary teachers a lot longer to make sub plans because they have to plan for an entire day as opposed to just one or two "preps."

What It Looks Like

When you become a principal (or even an assistant principal), you need to recognize that you have a lot to learn about the professionals in your building. When you take the time to listen to and learn from the teachers in your charge, it will go a long way to earning credibility with them. And it will certainly help you to make stronger decisions down the road. Carmen Maring, a middle school principal in Michigan, was a counselor prior to becoming a principal. She had never even been a teacher! Imagine the vulnerability involved in making *that* professional leap. When describing that transition to me, she was keenly aware of her struggle, as she lamented: "How can you be an instructional leader when you've never even been a teacher?" In her journey to become an instructional leader, she acknowledged that nobody is going to do it perfectly, but you have to be brave enough to take risks. She stressed, however, that these are "calculated risks, so that when you fail, you are failing forward." She also described it as "risking forward."

One principal talked to me about the results of giving anonymous surveys to teachers. If you have ever been on the receiving end of anonymous surveys, you understand the risk involved. Vulnerability is a prerequisite for this exercise. She said that teachers gave her high marks in some areas like her responsiveness to emails, but they were critical of her having her cell phone with her everywhere. She confessed to me her frustration with that critique: "How do you think I can respond to your emails?" Even though she felt like she had good reasons for having her cell phone (like responding to teacher emails more efficiently), she took the feedback to heart and made a concerted effort to put her phone up around teachers.

Shannon McCaskey talked to me about her commitment to being a servant leader to her faculty. "You're acknowledging that you don't have the answers… I like to show them that, hey, I'm willing to dig deep, get down and get dirty just like you. I've been there you know; I've been where you are, especially when they're going through trials in the classroom where they don't know the answer, they have no idea how to fix it… they need to see you were once there." She continued: "I tell them all the time that I have to apologize to my first classroom when I see those kids. I'm like, I'm so sorry! I did not know what I was doing." That is the type of vulnerability that endears you to your staff!

The principal, Chris Jackson, explained it to me bluntly: "You can't always be the smartest guy in the room." He began his career at the secondary level but quickly understood the importance of humility when he found himself leading amazing elementary teachers. "You may be pretty good with people as a principal, but you can't possibly know everything. I mean, the number of reps that our K-2 teachers have with teaching reading, like, how am I ever going to compete with that?"

Maybe you were a former PE teacher. Maybe you spent much of your career in the ranks of coaches. Maybe you were a chemistry teacher who just taught with a laser-like focus on your own discipline and you don't feel well rounded, academically speaking. That's okay! Don't pretend to have experience that you do not yet have, knowledge that you have not yet acquired, or skills that you have not yet mastered. Your staff probably already knows your background, so be candid with them about your learning curve. They will appreciate your transparency and vulnerability as you model for them a commitment to learning about the instructional program. And vulnerability is not just for the newbies who are just scratching the surface of their learning curve. It should not diminish as you progress throughout your career. Recall the "Dunning Kruger" effect that Fast talked about. She explained, "The more confident you are, the more humble you become, and the more you are willing to admit that there's things that you have to learn… It's just that the more competent and knowledgeable someone becomes, the more they realize they don't know." She relayed the recent experience of mentoring a young administrator. During his second year, she remarked to him that she could tell he was becoming more confident. He asked her how she could tell. "I said, because you're a lot more humble. You're telling me you don't know things."

A fear of vulnerability can be the obstacle to the bold curiosity discussed in Chapter 1. Fast talked about the importance of being willing to deal with the discomfort that might follow honest questions. Asking questions implies that you don't necessarily have all the answers. Asking questions involves a risk that you might encounter some uncomfortable answers. As she explained to me, "We sometimes avoid turning over the rocks when we don't want to find out what's underneath them." This takes a level of personal security that not all school leaders possess. But we need the courage to ask tough questions, and as she put it, "accept the messiness." Blink (2007) underscores the need for candid investigation this way:

> Everyone on the team must be willing to look at and analyze the data—no matter what the data suggest. If, for example, the data suggest that students in a high school are performing at lower levels in reading since the implementation of the block schedule three years ago, then the concept of block scheduling needs to be examined to a deeper level… The high school principal who has sung the praises of the block schedule to the members of the school board and the community must be willing to take a deeper look at the program based on the analysis of data. Emotional ties to programs and people must be checked at the door… (27–28)

I want to conclude this chapter with two final thoughts on how the leader's vulnerability translates into a more effective school. First, I want to refer back to the "Balanced Leadership Framework" (Rouleau, 2021). The leadership quality that had the second highest positive correlation to student achievement was "Adaptability" or "Flexibility." The description of this trait read: "Adapts his or her leadership behavior to the needs of the current situation and is comfortable with dissent" (4). The opposite approach to this type of leadership, of course, would be "My way or the highway!" It takes vulnerability to be willing to adjust your own plans or to acknowledge that a course of action is needed other than the one with which you might be most comfortable. Moreover, insecure leaders are not comfortable with dissent. They may view disagreements as a challenge to their authority and a threat to their leadership. Leaders characterized by humility don't take the dissent personally, and they are willing to adjust course for the good of the school.

Second, consider what it means to trust someone, and the vulnerability that is embedded in the notion of giving up control. Giving trust involves a degree of risk. When you trust, you give up control. In the school building, principals have the opportunity to extend trust to their teachers when they give them autonomy in the classroom. I can say from first-hand experience that this is one of the things teachers appreciate most from their administration. When I interviewed the teacher Tracy Colley, this is one of the first things she mentioned. She valued autonomy in the classroom. Daniel Pink wrote the best seller, *Drive* (2011), in which he synthesized decades of research about what motivates human behavior. He found that one of the most salient factors that motivate people in their work is the extent to which they have autonomy in their job. Cotton's review of the research around principals and student achievement (2003) also highlighted the value of teacher autonomy: "Principals of effective schools respect their teachers' skills and judgment, and allow them considerable autonomy in organizing and managing their classrooms" (70). This autonomy does not mean that principals are detached from the classroom or disengaged with instructional practices as she explains, "The research on principals of high-achieving schools finds that they are more involved in teachers' instructional practice *yet at the same time* they allow teachers more instructional autonomy than principals do in less-effective schools" (32).

Vulnerability is not about relishing weakness or wallowing in inadequacy; it's about being honest about your own limitations, being transparent about your learning curve, and moving forward with humility. Your vulnerability will earn you the respect of your staff, and it will allow you to lead more authentically. Your teachers need to see you as human, warts and all. They already know you're a flawed leader. (Trust me on this one!) But the humility you demonstrate while leading them will strengthen your impact.

Questions for Reflection

Am I honest with myself about my own personal and professional weaknesses?

What are the things that I feel threatened by?

What are the barriers to my own vulnerability?

What are the things that keep me from leading with transparency?

To what extent am I predictable?

When are the times that I view vulnerability as a weakness or a liability?

What are the factors that prevent my staff from being vulnerable?

Am I comfortable being vulnerable with my superintendent?

Are there things that you should be asking your district office for help on?

What could be some strategies for addressing your own insecurities?

References

Blink, R. J. (2007). *Data-Driven Instructional Leadership*. Routledge.

Cawelti, G. (1993). Foreword. In R. Goldhammer, R. H. Anderson, & R. J. Krajewski (Eds.), *Clinical Supervision: Special Methods for the Supervision of Teachers* (3rd ed.). Harcourt Brace Jovanovich.

Cotton, K. (2003). *Principals and Student Achievement: What the Research Says*. ASCD.

DeWitt, P. (2020). *Instructional Leadership: Creating Practice out of Theory*. Corwin.

Glickman, C., Gordon, S., & Ross-Gordon, J. (2010). *Supervision and Instructional Leadership: A Developmental Approach*. Pearson.

Pink, D. (2011). *Drive: The Surprising Truth About What Motivates Us*. Riverhead Books.

Rouleau, K. (2021). *Balanced Leadership for Student Learning: A 2021 Update of McREL's Research-Based School Leadership Development Program*. McREL International.

4

Leading Without Relationships Isn't Leading

Anytime someone asks me about the biggest lesson I have learned in school administration, I tell the same story. In the spring of 2004, I was finishing up my third year as an assistant principal and my second year at Tarrant High School. I couldn't wait to take the next step and lead my own school. With three years of administration under my belt, I was sure I was ready. My principal announced he was retiring, so I was going to get my chance. At some point in the application process, I remember driving back from a meeting with my principal, and he said: "Danny, I think some of the teachers see you more as an advocate for students than for teachers." I couldn't believe my ears. I responded something like, "Of course I'm an advocate for students! They're the ones who need us! The adults can take care of themselves!" What I thought would be a badge of honor—advocating for kids—was actually being held against me. I couldn't believe it.

As you can guess, I did not get the job. The guy who became the next principal of Tarrant High School was in fact more qualified than me, and he did a great job. I was his assistant principal for two more years at that school and then four more years at a larger high school when he moved on. He became a trusted friend and valued mentor throughout my career. So it worked out in the end. But in the summer of 2004, I did a lot of soul searching about how I viewed my role in administration. I experienced what I would call a "paradigm shift" with respect to how I approached my job. As educators, we get into the profession to make a difference for kids. What I realized is that when one makes the leap to administration, the focus has to change. The new goal is to make a difference for teachers. Of course, leaders still need to hold on to their love for kids and continue to connect with them, but I firmly believe that the focus of school leaders needs to be on their teachers—connecting with them, supporting them, valuing them. That priority is the focus of this chapter.

Oftentimes, administrators can view instructional leadership in the context of their role as a supervisor. It is true that administrators supervise the teachers under their charge; this conception can imply a top-down view of the relationship between administrator and teacher. While this may be the conventional model of instructional leadership, I don't think it is the most effective way of conceptualizing it or practicing it. Gordon (1997) describes a different approach to instructional leadership:

> *A paradigm shift toward the collegial model includes the following:*
>
> 1. A collegial rather than a hierarchical relationship between teachers and formally designated supervisors
> 2. Supervision as the province of teachers as well as formally designated supervisors
> 3. A focus on teacher growth rather than teacher compliance
> 4. Facilitation of teachers collaborating with each other in instructional improvement efforts
> 5. Teacher involvement in ongoing reflective inquiry. (116)

You'll recall from the introduction that the familiar saying, "They don't care how much you know until they know how much you care," applies to principals. Winning over the teachers is a prerequisite for effective instructional leadership. So get to know your teachers! Kafele talks about building the type of culture where "your presence as an instructional leader is welcomed by your staff." Carrier (2017) reiterates the point, writing, "Leaders sincerely are about those they lead at a personal level and are committed to developing a positive relationship with them. This type of focus can be best described as attending to issues of the heart…" (59).

What It Looks Like

Ashley Bowling has meetings at the beginning and end of year with teachers, asking about their needs for communication, support, etc. "not about data, but about how you are as a person." Jennifer Hogan does a "Friday check-in" via a Google Form that teachers are asked to fill out each week. While not everybody fills it out, it's a chance for them to share about their week. "They can say it was a tough one, but I'm looking forward to the next one. Or it wasn't so good, or I need a little TLC." It's also a chance for teachers to ask questions to the administration. Hogan works at a large school, so this is a good way for the administration to get a pulse on the building.

There are countless ways to make connections with teachers. There is not a formula for building relationships, but it begins with making it a priority. And it's important that you genuinely care about them. When I began one of my principalships, I remember teachers talking to me about how much they appreciated the fact that one of their previous principals knew their children's names and would consistently ask about how they are doing. It's hard to overstate how much teachers appreciate leaders who care about them as people. Leaders who have cultivated strong relationships with their teachers are able to share in the joy of a graduate degree, a new baby, or a spouse's promotion. But principals who know their staff also understand the myriad of outside factors that can have a negative impact on the wellbeing of their teachers. Teachers experience depression, divorce, the loss of a family member, the stress of caring for an elderly parent. It's important that school leaders are aware of these dynamics and demonstrate empathy and compassion toward their teachers throughout the school year. These types of principals are the ones that teachers truly value, as described by Carrier (2017) who interviewed many principals in preparation for her own book on instructional leadership:

> They all describe that they felt they could trust the principal to look out for their best interest, the best interest of students, and the best interest of the school as a whole. In short, the instructional leaders in the study were perceived as caring about the people in their school's community in what was perceived by the teachers as a real and substantial way. These teachers did not discuss how well a principal analyzed data or to what level they were involved in maintaining a focus on learning when asked about their principals practiced instructional leadership; but instead described their principals as individuals with whom they had positive, supportive, trust-based relationships. (60)

Jon Wennstrom took pride in being a "relationship guy," but he stressed to me in our conversation that your relationships with your teachers cannot be transactional. As he put it, "I'm not going to walk in and check on how somebody's doing if I'm going to ask them to cover a room for me in the afternoon… or I have some bad news to share." It's important to connect with your teachers for the value of connecting with them. If teachers see you coming down the hall toward them, and one remarks to their colleague, "Oh… there's Dr. Steele. I wonder what he wants…" that is not a good sign, and it's not a reputation that a principal should want to earn.

    I have told many aspiring administrators and young assistant principles that they will be defined by their ability to support their teachers. I learned that lesson the hard way when I didn't get that first principalship, and the truth of that admonition has been validated for me throughout my career. After that bitter disappointment in the summer of 2004, I worked for seven more years as an assistant principal where I had the opportunity to practice the skill and demonstrate my commitment to supporting teachers. Building a reputation for supporting teachers was one of my primary professional goals for the remainder of my career. Learning that tough lesson early on is what allowed me to write this in *Essential Truths for Principals* (Steele & Whitaker, 2019): "A principal's instructional leadership is only as strong as their commitment to supporting teachers" (4).

While school leaders are walking around, cultivating the relationships with staff members, it's important for them to be self-aware. One morning, while walking around the school, I stopped by the front desk in our main office to talk through a situation with our two secretaries. As I felt the conversation wrapping up, I began to leave, when they both confronted me… seemingly simultaneously. (It's almost like they had conspired… "Ok… the next time Dr. Steele walks by, let's say something!") They began something like this: "Dr. Steele, sometimes we'll be talking to you, and then you'll just walk off in the middle of the conversation." I was stunned… "Wait… what? Surely I can't be that rude." They chuckled. "We assume you have other things to do, or you're thinking about something else." I responded: "Well I'm sorry for doing that; that's terrible! I think that maybe what's happening is that in my mind, I have closure in the conversation… so then I'm moving on to my next task, conversation, meeting, etc. … but maybe y'all didn't have closure yet. I'm truly sorry, and I'll try to be more aware." They smiled. The conversation was all in good spirit. But I was definitely taken back. That evening, after a school program, I happened to be leaving the school with my three assistant principals, so I decided to relay the earlier conversation with the ladies in the front office… just to get their read on the issue. As soon as I finished, they all began laughing. One of them quipped, "Danny, we've just all gotten used to that already." She went on, "If you mentioned this to the teachers, they would laugh too!" It turns out, I had a significant blindspot in how I interacted with others. It sounds crazy as I write this, but I was not always aware when a conversation was actually over.

I had an occasion to talk to our teachers by grade level the next week, and I shared my experience with the ladies of the front office. And true enough, some teachers offered a "knowing" smile, or even a laugh. As I concluded my comments, I told the teachers, "So two things: first, if I've ever walked off in the middle of a conversation with you, I apologize. And second, if I ever am guilty of being so oblivious like that again, you have my permission to call me out on it."

The next day, I was walking the halls a few minutes before the tardy bell. The halls were full of students, and teachers were outside their doors, chatting with their colleagues. My oldest son had just texted me something, and I was trying to decide how to respond when I heard a voice 20 feet behind me. "Danny!" I whipped my head around, and a seventh grade English teacher who was in a group of other teachers, said: "I said 'good morning' when you walked by, and you didn't even acknowledge me!" She had taken me up on my offer the day before. I hustled over to the group of teachers to apologize. She said, "Oh… I figured you were thinking about your morning announcements." I responded, "Actually, I was preoccupied with what I was going to text my son… but I'm sorry! I shouldn't have been that distracted… and thank you for saying something to me." We all laughed. I was trying to work on being more self-aware. And I had an "inside joke" with my colleagues. This may sound corny, but I viewed these experiences as a sort of bonding moment with some of my staff.

We all have blindspots in our relationships. Consider what your blindspots might be in how you interact with your staff. And do you have colleagues who will have the courage to point them out to you? I know I was guilty of being frequently distracted by my phone, and I am sure that is the case with many of those reading these words. Perhaps you listen to talk next. You are not totally focused on what the other person is saying; you are thinking through what your next comment will be. It is not unusual for principals to have favorite teachers, just like it is not unusual for teachers to have favorite students. (My favorite teachers were the ones who brought positive energy to work, demonstrated genuine care for the students, took pride in being an excellent teacher, and collaborated well with colleagues.) It could be tempting for administrators to focus too much time connecting with their "superstars" and not enough time connecting with other teachers. Just like we don't want teachers teaching to one side of the classroom and focusing on the students who always raise their hands, we need school leaders to devote time to building those professional and collegial relationships with every teacher in the building.

Benefits of Strong Relationships

Every principal that I interviewed for this book talked about the importance of relationships, and that was no surprise to me. As a rule of thumb, principals have risen to that position because they have demonstrated proficiency (if not excellence) in connecting with people. I actually don't think I can imagine a more prerequisite skill. I've observed faculties where the teachers resented the administrators and there was an "us against them" mentality that was pervasive. That is obviously toxic. Strong relationships between teachers and administrators, in contrast, go a long way toward building a strong school culture. It fosters higher staff morale which leads to smaller turnover of staff. There is a common adage that "employees don't leave jobs; they leave managers." Leaders who foster strong connections with their people inspire loyalty. The relationships provide the foundation for any type of leadership, by cultivating trust. Jennifer Hogan talked to me about how strong relationships and the sense of trust contribute to a culture of high expectations. "If we're going to demand that our teachers have high expectations for our students, we have to have high expectations for our teachers too. Sometimes that means sharing constructive feedback. That means asking them to challenge what they're doing, what their processes are in the classroom, and that is not going to be received well or acted on without trust."

Instructional leadership does not happen without good relationships and without a culture of trust. Jim Collins (2005) noted, "True leadership only exists if people follow when they have the freedom not to" (13). So what compels people to follow a leader when they have the freedom not to? At many job interviews I remember telling the committee, "Before teachers buy into my vision for the school, they have to first buy into me." Teachers buy in when you build those relationships.

Questions for Reflection

Do I know who and what each of my teachers cares about outside of school?

Who are the teachers on my staff with whom I need to spend more time connecting?

What are my blindspots as I interact with adults in my school?

Who on my staff will be honest with me about what my blindspots are?

Are there systems or habits I need to develop to prevent distractions while I engage with my staff? For example, do I need to start leaving my phone in my office when I walk the halls?

What is a simple way that I can connect with my teachers? For example, could I keep a list of all the staff birthdays and then text or email teachers on their special day?

Who are the teachers on my staff that I don't care for, and how could I begin to change my attitude toward them?

How approachable am I? Are there ways that I can become more approachable?

How can I spend more time listening than talking while interacting with my teachers?

Do you have staff members who will help keep you informed about important life events going on with teachers? (This might be an assistant principal, a secretary, or a teacher leader.)

References

Carrier, L. (2017). *Keeping the Leadership in Instructional Leadership: Developing Your Practice*. Routledge.

Collins, J. (2005). *Good to Great and the Social Sectors: A Monograph to Accompany Good to Great*. Jim Collins.

Gordon, S.P. (1997). Has the field of supervision evolved to a point that it should be called something else? Yes. In J. Glanz and R.F. Neville (Eds.), *Educational Supervision: Perspectives, issues, and controversies* (114–123). Christopher-Gordon Publishers.

Steele, D., & Whitaker, T. (2019). *Essential Truths for Principals*. Routledge.

5

Creating Opportunities for Growth

Instructional leadership is not something we do *to* teachers; it is a way of leading that creates value *for* teachers *with* teachers. This chapter represents what most school leaders likely view as the primary function of instructional leadership—engaging in work that results in teachers becoming more effective. Smith and Andrews (1989) wrote, "The most obvious role of the principal as an instructional resource is to facilitate good teaching" (12). The seed I want to plant with readers, however, is that this process is fundamentally not about principals imparting expertise to teachers. I wrote in *Essential Truths for Principals*, "Instructional leadership is not about improving teachers; it is about creating the conditions where teachers can improve themselves" (Steele & Whitaker, 2019, p. 3). In this chapter I highlight two ways that school leaders can facilitate improvements with instructional practices: through having strategic conversations with teachers that provide opportunities to reflect on their practice, and through creating opportunities for teachers to learn from each other.

Strategic Conversations

According to Smith and Andrews (1989, p. 12), "The most obvious role of the principal as an instructional resource is to facilitate good teaching." This past year, the well-known author and speaker Baruti Kafele released *What Is My Value Instructionally to the Teachers I Supervise?* (2025). I was excited to read it as I prepared for writing my own book on the topic. In his book, he places particular focus on the school leader as a "coach." He introduces it with the following scenario:

> It's game day in a high school football locker room on a Friday evening in September. The coaches have been preparing the team all week for the game and providing them with powerful messaging. The big day is now here. The team is excited, pumped, and ready to take to the field. But right before it's time to go out onto the field, the head coach gathers the team together for a final motivational message. After the message he yells out, "Let's get this win!" The team responds with a loud "Let's go!" And as the team begins to run onto the field, the coach yells, "Guys, if you need me or any of the assistant coaches, we'll be here in the locker room. Don't hesitate to come back and reach out to us." The players then run out onto the field to play the game, and the coaches remain in the locker room. (1)

Kafele uses this absurd scenario to underscore the point that principals need to remain fully engaged with their teachers during the school year, providing meaningful feedback to them to empower them to excel in their craft. While popping into classrooms can help with culture and visibility, it is not enough in and of itself to improve the practice of teachers. He argues that teachers actually need to receive feedback on their practice. Principals have hopefully accumulated a measure of expertise and wisdom in their training and as a result of their own experiences, and they need to have the courage to share it strategically with their faculty. Please note that "strategically" is the operative word in that last sentence. So what does it mean to share or "coach" strategically? Like every great metaphor, this one has its limits. Consider the ways that Kafele's poignant scenario might break down. First, football coaches have total control over playing time. So players who are not sufficiently receptive to the coaching probably won't make it off the bench. For all practical purposes, principals do not have that type of leverage over their teachers. While young teachers who are not responsive to the coaching of their administration (and do not have some sort of job security) can be let go at the end of the year, it rarely happens during the school year. And with the exception of some sort of gross dereliction of duty, it is also rare for a teacher to be let go once they have achieved a version of "tenure," Second, there is a salient level of disparity between the expertise of varsity football coaches and their teenage players that is not analogous to the expertise gap that may or may not exist between a principal and teacher. Consider for example a young principal who was a former PE teacher, attempting to coach a high school chemistry teacher. It's not hard to imagine an "expertise gap" that significantly undermines the credibility of the principal. Does this mean that the principal does not have the right to provide feedback on the chemistry lesson? Of course not. There are sound instructional practices that transcend disciplines. It doesn't require a knowledge of chemistry to identify if students are engaged in the chemistry lesson. But coaching teachers who are not receptive is an act of futility. And even worse, it can actually be counterproductive. Being strategic about coaching teachers entails an understanding of the need to lead with vulnerability and lead with relationships. Effective instructional leaders recognize their own limitations and are humble about the things they don't know and the experiences they have not had. And they are committed to cultivating relationships. Before teachers buy into the leadership of their principal they have to first buy into them as people. When school leaders lead and act in the light of this reality, they earn the respect of their teachers, and ensure that those teachers are more responsive to their coaching. Kafele reminds school leaders of the myriad of resources that teachers have available to aid in their professional learning including "conferences, institutes, academies, seminars, lectures, presentations, podcasts, livestreams, videos, modules, books, journals, blogs, and learning networks / social media" (3). But he emphasizes that none of these resources can provide direct feedback on their lesson. This is why principals who take the time to observe teachers and provide feedback can play a strong role in the process of fostering the professional growth of their faculty. When principals observe teachers, it is often in the context of a chaotic day. Whether the observation is part of a formal evaluation or just an informal pop in, it is easy to shortchange the most valuable part of the process. As principals are often strapped for time, it is tempting to cut corners with the post-conference. Smith and Andrews (1989) write, "The principal's ability to help teachers expand their use of instructional strategies is key to improving the school. The primary, and maybe the only, place that the principal has the opportunity to improve instruction is during a conference with a teacher after a clinical observation of a teaching episode" (33). And Glickman et al. (2010) describes research that shows "Teachers who receive the most classroom feedback are also most satisfied with teaching" (288). In this sense, providing feedback to teachers doesn't just improve practice; it improves morale.

Glickman et al. (2010) explain that "Observation is a two-part process—first *describing* what has been seen and then *interpreting* what it means" (237). They further note that "observations should be used as a base of information to create an instructional dialogue between supervisor and teacher" (237). They describe the observation process as a "mirror" (256) to facilitate a process of self-reflection. When administrators debrief with teachers about a lesson, it is an opportunity to ask strategic questions that prompt this self-reflection. This is what it means to hold up a "mirror" for the teachers. The questions administrators choose to ask reflects the values they hope to underscore. For example:

- ♦ When they ask a question about the focus of the lesson, they are highlighting the role of the curriculum.
- ♦ When they ask a question about instructional strategies, they are highlighting the importance of intentionality.

- When they ask a question about the work students were doing, they are highlighting the significance of engagement.
- When they ask a question about plans for academic intervention, they are highlighting the value of all students learning.
- When they ask a question about differentiation, they are highlighting the unique needs of students.
- When they ask a question about plans for assessment, they're highlighting the significance of gauging the mastery of the learning objectives, as well as the evaluation of instructional effectiveness.

In my experience, this type of approach with teachers—sort of a Socratic dialogue—has proven to be the most well received and the most effective when talking with teachers about their instructional practice.

Teachers Learning from Teachers

One of the things I loved about being a school administrator is that I had the privilege of seeing great teachers all over the school. Formal workshops and conferences can be an important component of one's professional development, but I am convinced the greatest source of professional growth can be achieved just by learning from the expert down the hall. There is amazing talent, creativity, and innovation occurring on a daily basis in each one of our schools! But many teachers are not aware of the great instructional practices that are happening in their own building. Furthermore, they don't always feel comfortable venturing into another teacher's "turf." Observing a peer seems awkward to many teachers. But in a great school, every teacher is a mentor! Every teacher has skills, knowledge, activities, strategies, ideas, or wisdom to offer to their colleagues. I think one of the important goals of school leaders should be to foster the type of school culture that promotes mutual respect among colleagues and explicitly recognizes the reality that every teacher has something to offer to their fellow teachers and then creates opportunities for teachers to learn from one another.

What It Looks Like

As an assistant principal, I was working in a school with amazing teachers. I wanted to figure out a way for them to observe each other. So I sent an email to the faculty outlining my "expert down the hall" initiative. Eighteen teachers responded to my email indicating an interest in visiting another classroom. I paid for three subs, and they would rotate to cover a different class each period. For an investment of about $300, we were able to facilitate 18 teachers observing their colleagues. I received overwhelmingly positive feedback.

Carmen Maring talked about the importance of empowering her teachers to contribute to staff meetings. She posed the question to me: "How do we open the doors and lower the walls so that people next to them know what they're doing too?" The first core teacher I ever hired as a principal was a guy named Chris Myles June of 2011. He was a quality teacher, but he soon moved into administration. He is currently working at the district level, and I was recently on a zoom conversation with him where he relayed to me a story from his days as a principal. I found it so inspiring, I asked him to email it to me. His account follows:

> *To start, it is important to note that the idea started due to the COVID pandemic. We were coming out of COVID but some fears were still very much alive. Teachers were isolated in their classrooms. Some didn't feel comfortable coming out of their rooms, while others weren't sure how welcomed they would be in another teacher's classroom. Out of respect for their colleagues they remained isolated. I understood and totally respected it, but in the back of my mind I knew how important it was not to become isolated as a teacher… it can get lonely.*
>
> *At the beginning of the 2021 school year, our new instructional coordinator began reintroducing instructional rounds. However,*

due to the substitute shortage we couldn't send teachers from building to building. The solution was for the principals to do instructional rounds at designated schools. The goal was to hopefully take something back and share it with our own faculty. My school was not selected this particular year as a school that would be visited. As I visited other schools, I began to have a better understanding of the rockstars I had in my own building and the brainstorming began to showcase my people.

At the beginning of the 2022 school year, our instructional rounds continued but we had more of a focus on vertical rounds within our zones. The goal was to focus on aligning the curriculum across grade levels, especially through major transitions such as 6th grade and 9th grade.

Going into the 2023 school year, my school still had not been selected as a school to host instructional rounds. At this point, I had had two years of seeing great things in other schools but our school was still struggling to find substitutes to cover classrooms. Our teachers were doing a better job at sharing the great things taking place in their classrooms. I was being invited to several classrooms a month and I was blown away at the things our students were producing.

During a back to school administration meeting with my team, I shared my thoughts and overall vision on this topic. I have to shout out my team here. I had an amazing team of assistant principals who could listen to my big picture thoughts and then come up with strategies to make my vision applicable in the classroom. Literally one day after sharing this information about finding ways to get our teachers out of their room and seeing other teachers, my AP's brought the idea to me that transformed into Eagle Days.

Eagle Days were developed as a strategy method to encourage our teachers to visit other classrooms inside our own building to see the incredible work being done by other colleagues. We simply printed giant eagle heads (our mascot) on blue paper (school color) and laminated them. We gave them to every teacher and told them when they were doing something cool, innovative,

> *different, engaging, etc. and they were comfortable with other teachers coming in and seeing the lesson, then we wanted them to post their blue eagle head on their door outside their classroom. The sign basically has a meaning of "come in and see what we are doing." The initiative started slow but quickly gained speed. To start, we pulled a small group of teachers in and explained our idea and gathered their input and tweaked a few things. After that, I had an AP sell the idea at a faculty meeting. A month later at our next faculty meeting, I shared a designated date that would be considered Eagle Day and I encouraged our teachers to develop a lesson that they felt they would like others to see. I also asked them to email me if they were planning to participate along with the lesson's topic and standard it was addressing. I then invited our district leadership to come and visit my school and my teachers on this day (I didn't tell the teachers about this because I didn't know who would show up). My team and I were blown away by the response we got from our faculty willing to participate. The following district leaders showed up and visited classrooms: Superintendent, Deputy Superintendent of Instruction, Coordinator of Instruction, and all of our Instructional Coaches. My teachers loved being able to show off their talents and the skills of their students!! We debriefed with the faculty the next month and the faculty came up with the idea that Eagle Days should be an everyday thing, not just designated to a particular day. Since then Eagles have been posted outside classroom doors as teachers feel comfortable.*

I would further note that he told me "Eagle Days" spawned a number of other cool initiatives in his school including vertical administrative swap, teacher classroom swap, a mental health career fair by Peerhelpers, and a student career fair led by the Future Business Leaders of America.

Shannon McCaskey makes a point of holding her faculty meetings in a different classroom every time and uses it as an opportunity to showcase that teacher's practices. An activity like that not only validates the host teacher, but it introduces the entire faculty to new ideas. McCaskey's commitment to creating shared practices in her school was abundantly evident through our conversation. She put it this way: "I'm not impressed when one teacher in four is crushing it in a professional learning community. I'm impressed when that teacher shares what they're doing…"

Annette Sanchez developed a culture of teachers coaching one another and being specific about what they learned from one another. She realized that her veteran teachers could play a vital role in modeling lessons for the younger teachers in their professional learning community time, explaining, "During our Thursday meetings, the teacher leaders would teach Monday's lesson for the teachers. They would go through the lesson, talk about some of the misconceptions that students had, and then walk them through the rest of the week."

When I was working on my dissertation over 20 years ago I was confronted with one of the dynamics that poses a challenge to principals providing instructional leadership. Professional growth for a teacher typically happens in a context of vulnerability. Teachers need to be willing to step outside of their comfort zone. Common sense tells us that it is easier to be vulnerable with a colleague than with the administrator who is also doing our evaluation. Glickman et al. (2010) underscore this reality discussing the value of peer coaching:

> Since teachers naturally turn to each other for help more often than to a supervisor, and since supervision is concerned primarily with improving instruction rather than with summative evaluation (renewal of contracts), teachers helping teachers has become a formalized and well-received way of ensuring direct assistance to every staff member. (294)

The principal, Chris Jackson, candidly admitted to me, "They like listening to each other more than me." Jennifer Brown, the 2016 Alabama Teacher of the Year, worked to create a more collaborative culture within her own school by initiating structured peer observations. In my book *The Total Teacher* (2022) she recounted the experience:

> About 12 years into my teaching career, a colleague and I began discussing the need to see other teachers in their classrooms. After much discussion, we were determined to establish a teacher-led system of instructional rounds at our school, even if we were the only two participants. After an overwhelming response from our faculty, we implemented Leading by Learning teacher-led instructional rounds so that our teachers could learn and grow together. Small groups of teachers observe other teachers' lessons and upon leaving the room, the groups reflected on the lessons and discussed methods of implementation in their own classrooms. (105)

This program proved to be a great success in the school and was a source of inspiration for the teachers involved.

I'll add a note of caution here. The importance of authentic feedback to teachers is what came through when I interviewed Karissa Lang. She went so far as to say, "I feel like we have ruined principals by doing instructional rounds." She explained that teachers have become so conditioned to jumping through some of the hoops identified on the formal checklists carried round by the observers—things like having a "can do" statement written on the board—that both observers and teachers can become a bit disconnected from the actual engagement of the learners. She quipped, "You can get up there and teach your pants off, but if the kids aren't engaged, then what have you done?" I realize that school leaders have utilized feedback forms and checklists with great success as they visit classrooms; it's just important to remember feedback should always be genuine, personal, and practical.

When you see an amazing activity in a classroom, let others know. I remember numerous times over my career when I observed something cool in a classroom and then went and covered another teacher's classroom for five minutes so they could witness their colleague in action. When you do this, you build bridges between your teachers and get them out of the silos in which teachers often operate. When you hear good ideas, pass them along. If you come across some new research, make it available to the faculty. If someone tells you an inspiring story, share it at the next staff meeting. As you have conversations with teachers, whether informally in the hallway, or formally in a post-conference, be mindful of the values that you are promoting and the strategic way that you foster self-reflection. And be intentional about amplifying the great work of your teachers. Create as many opportunities as possible for teachers to learn from and inspire one another. This is the type of environment where teachers will thrive and grow as practitioners.

Questions for Reflection

What are the most strategic ways to share ideas, activities, or research with your faculty?

What are the values that I care about when talking with teachers about their instruction?

What are the most strategic ways for me to promote self-reflection with my teachers?

How do you create opportunities for your best teachers to share ideas with their colleagues?

What would it take to facilitate peer observations with your teachers?

What are the barriers to teachers observing their colleagues in our school?

What are strategic ways to engage with teachers who are not comfortable with colleagues visiting their classroom?

Are there adequate structures and routines in place to ensure consistent and meaningful collaboration among teachers?

How do I know the collaboration is valuable?

Which of my teachers are the best at connecting with colleagues, and how can I do more to leverage their strengths?

Are any of my teachers operating in a silo or on an island? Why is that? How could I help to build a bridge between that teacher and their colleagues?

Do all of our teachers feel like they have something to contribute to their colleagues?

References

Glickman, C., Gordon, S., & Ross-Gordon, J. (2010). *Supervision and Instructional Leadership: A Developmental Approach*. Pearson.

Kafele, B. (2025). *What Is My Value Instructionally to the Teachers I Supervise?* ASCD.

Smith, W. F., & Andrews, R. L. (1989). *Instructional Leadership: How Principals Make a Difference*. ASCD.

Steele, D. (2022). *The Total Teacher: Understanding the Three Dimensions that Define Effective Educators*. Routledge.

Steele, D., & Whitaker, T. (2019). *Essential Truths for Principals*. Routledge.

6

Delegating Is Winning

Principals sometimes feel like they need to be all things to all people. It is not possible. It is also not possible to know everything you need to know to lead a school or do all that needs to be done to lead a school. There is an African proverb which says "It takes a village to raise a child." In some ways, it takes a village to lead a school. It might be hard for some principals to let go of some of their authority, and it may be challenging for some school leaders to acknowledge their own inadequacy, but this is where the courage to be vulnerable comes in handy. It allows principals to embrace the role of "the village." DeWitt (2020) writes, "The goal of an instructional leader is to lower our own status as a principal and raise the status of those around us. It involves creating spaces of dialogue around learning to respect the expertise of the teacher" (72). Whether it is through delegating managerial tasks that allow for you to spend more time in classrooms, involving teacher leaders who bring unique curricular expertise, or through sharing decision making with staff members, principals who involve their colleagues in the leadership and operation of the school create a stronger instructional program.

Recognize and Appreciate the Expertise Around You

There is a saying in management that you should "hire people smarter than you, and get out of their way." Without question, the most important thing a principal can do for their school is hire great teachers, but as I mentioned in the introduction, that is not the focus of this book. This chapter highlights the value of recognizing and capitalizing on the expertise already on staff. To be clear, this strategy is about being intentional and strategic with how you delegate.

In earlier chapters, we talked about the importance of being self-aware—of being honest about one's own strengths and weaknesses. Most new principals did not step into their role with a comprehensive understanding of all the disciplines in their school. I taught history for eight years before I became an administrator. I had no background in teaching math, language arts, science, physical education, foreign languages, fine arts, or career tech. I interviewed several principals who took on leadership roles in schools that were on a different level from the rest of their experience—someone with experience in high school who became an elementary school principal, for example. Unless you were a math teacher, it's a good bet that there are adults in the building who know more about teaching math than you do. Throughout my career I had the privilege of working with many amazing teachers. Some of them were quite vocal, collaborative, and invested in moving their curriculum and their colleagues in the right direction. Why would I not take advantage of their expertise, experience, and wisdom? Why would I not want their contribution? In a 2014 blog post DeWitt states, "If school leaders do not involve teachers in the process of being an instructional leader, they're really not leading at all." I wrote in *Essential Truths for Principals* (Steele & Whitaker, 2019), "The best leaders are not the ones with all the good ideas, they are the ones who capitalize on the good ideas of others" (35). And as Jon Wennstrom told me, "If someone's coming to me with an idea, it's probably going to take off…"

For starters, it begins with knowing your people, understanding their strengths, and appreciating their passions. And as I suggested in the last chapter, I think it's a good thing to assume that everyone on the faculty has strengths that can be tapped into. As the principal Ed Cosentino put it, "Everybody brings something to the table." So how do you know which teachers you can tap into? Certainly it's a matter of identifying qualities like expertise and passion, but as Jon Wennstrom explained, it's also about knowing who has "social capital" in your building. Know which teachers connect well with their colleagues. Understand which teachers are respected by their peers. Recognize which teachers are able to build consensus. In leadership, it's not enough to have the right idea. You have to be able to communicate that idea and effectively mobilize others to pursue it with you.

What It Looks Like

Leveraging the Expertise

In one of my schools, both the administration and the teachers had come to the realization our master schedule had some deficiencies. The most salient one was that we did not have enough time embedded into the day to provide academic intervention for students who were struggling. After consulting with our district office, we began a months-long review of the strengths and weaknesses of our schedule as well as what other options were. We looked at the schedules of other schools, and we analyzed the strengths and weaknesses of the various options. Here's the thing: I was not the engine that drove this effort. Sure, I talked about it at staff meetings, I sent emails about it, and I had many one-on-one conversations about it; but it was Reba Hudson, one of my assistant principals that led this effort. Reba loved curriculum and instruction, she had a keen eye toward data, and she loved to problem solve. She understood the challenges of our schedule intimately because she was the one having to schedule students into their intervention classes. She understood the reality of students missing core instruction for the sake of intervention because she lived with it on a daily basis.

It is hard for me to overstate how much time she spent working on a new schedule and continuously tweaking it to make it better.

She would share drafts with me. We would share drafts with the central office. We would share them in staff meetings and ask for their feedback. Over the months, the schedule went through countless iterations, as she worked to incorporate the feedback of teachers. She worked on it during the day. She worked on it at night. She worked on it while flying on an airplane. I remember her texting one night that she had a "fix" for a flaw that a teacher had identified in a staff meeting earlier that day. She was relentless, and I could not have been more proud of her. Or thankful! Reba worked hard on this project, but she also loved it. She was passionate about what she was doing.

Leaders need to recognize when they are not the ones to lead a project. They need to acknowledge that they might not have the knowledge, skills, passion, or credibility to drive the train. I'm reminded of a year when our school was launching a new "character" initiative. It was led by two of my assistant principals and a group of teachers. I understand the value of character education, but I did not have the same fire around this project as they did. So they led that charge and did a fantastic job. As one principal told me, "It's not just delegation; it's about allowing others to run with their own passions and ideas."

Adam Dovico, an elementary principal in North Carolina, relayed a story to me that exemplified strategic utilization of staff members. He told me the story of his school going through a focused implementation of Multi-Tiered System of Supports. They were deep into it with data collection and implementing tiered intervention to fidelity. His teachers saw the value, but there is only so much time in the day, and teachers can handle only so much on their plate. To alleviate the strain on his teachers, Adam had the idea of repurposing his paraprofessionals. These aides had traditionally been relegated to tasks like laminating, stapling, cutting, and making copies. What Adam did was to train them in the strategies the teachers were using, and then they were able to lead small groups and alleviate the burden on teachers with other sorts of intervention. A willingness to think outside the box and reimagine traditional roles allowed paraprofessionals to transform into "instructional assistants."

Increasing the Efficiency

Sometimes delegation is simply a matter of managing the school more efficiently. Carmen Maring talked to me about the fact that when she first stepped into her role, virtually every decision flowed through the principal's office. She recounted a time that someone came to her asking if she could set up a table in the hallway for lost and found. What she learned is that the previous principal kept a close eye on all the tables because of one being damaged at some point, and all the requests for tables were directed to the principal. Maring did not want to be buried in that type of administrivia, so she realized she needed to build capacity in others to make decisions—and then trust them to make those decisions. Kafele (2025) noted, "If your daily duties do not allow you to be the instructional leader that your students and staff need you to be, you have ongoing adjustments to make" (11). In *Shifting the Monkey* (2014), Todd Whitaker talks about the fact that leaders should not be doing things that others can do. Leaders have unique skill sets and should not take on jobs or roles that others can do effectively. Kafele didn't mince words when he asked: "Is cafeteria duty keeping you from being the instructional leader you need to be? If you are a principal, I will give you one lunch period per day to be in the cafeteria. Anything more is too much. You are the principal, and you have more important things to do beyond cafeteria duty" (39). Jon Wennstrom talked to me about utilizing the expertise of secretaries, custodians, and everyone else in the building. As he noted, "Those are people that carry a lot of weight in the building, and quite frankly, have expertise in a lot of areas that I don't have. And I need to lean on their support."

Sharing the Leadership

Ashley Bowling told me in our conversation: "I have learned that if I don't build leaders in the building, then I'm not leaving the impact I can as a principal." Jennifer Hogan talked about the importance of empowering her assistant principals and recruiting department chairs who had demonstrated the ability to lead their colleagues effectively. Annete Sanchez allowed her lead math and ELA teachers to provide models of professional learning communities.

There is a poignant adage that speaks to the power of collaboration: "The smartest person in the room is the room." During my years as a principal, I relied heavily on my building leadership team. In my work with principals now, this is a leadership structure which I routinely emphasize. Bring teachers on to your leadership team that care about the students, care about their craft, care about their colleagues, and care about the direction of the school. A team of teachers like that will never steer you wrong. (In addition to a cross section of teachers in the building, I think it's a good idea to include representatives from other groups in the school like support staff and counselors.) There were times that I could not meet with the entire leadership team as often as I liked because of scheduling conflicts, so I would meet with the team in smaller groups. Sometimes I would send the team an email to get their feedback on a decision I was considering. Often, I would talk to these team members individually during their planning period or informally in the hallway. Leading collaboratively will almost always result in stronger decisions and better buy-in from the staff. Not only does the leadership team help chart the direction for the school, but it can also be effective for helping you keep your finger on the pulse of the school. These teachers hear the grumblings from their neighbors down the hallway, and they are aware of unique challenges or questions that are confronting their colleagues, so they provide valuable intel to help you be as proactive as possible in addressing potential issues.

Principals have a tough job. But that job becomes more manageable, and the principal becomes more effective, when they allow others in the building to rise to the challenge of leading too. Max DePree wrote in *Leadership Jazz* (1992):

> I have come to realize that I have depended on followers for many things—spirit, commitment, inspiration, expertise. They are the ones who make a vision real, and at the very heart of leadership lies the necessity of making

it possible for followers to contribute. Followers need a chance to do their best; leaders need a lot of help. (110)

When leaders become proficient with delegating—when they are strategic with how they leverage the expertise of the adults in the school, students will inevitably benefit. And as a bonus, staff morale will increase. The adults will be more fulfilled in their job, knowing that their contributions are recognized and valued.

Questions for Reflection

What are my leadership strengths as relating to the instructional program?

What are my leadership weaknesses relating to the instructional program?

Do I know the strengths and interests of the teachers in our school?

Who are some people on our staff that I need to tap into?

What is it that prevents me from utilizing people on my staff?

Are there some management or operational activities that I could pass off to someone else and then have more time to spend with teachers?

Do our teachers feel like they share in the decision making of the school?

What are ways that our leadership team can be more involved in the life of the school?

What are tasks or responsibilities that the staff in our front office think I should let go of?

Are there things that I am currently doing that others in the school could do better or more efficiently?

References

DePree, M. (1992). *Leadership Jazz*. Dell Publishing.

DeWitt, P. (2014). Help! My Principal Says He's an Instructional Leader! *Peter DeWitt's Finding Common Ground* [blog]. http:/blogs.edweek.org/edweek/finding_common_ground/2014/08/help_my_principal_says_hes_an_instructinal_leader.html

DeWitt, P. (2020). *Instructional Leadership: Creating Practice out of Theory*. Corwin.

Kafele, B. (2025). *What Is My Value Instructionally to the Teachers I Supervise?* ASCD.

Steele, D., & Whitaker, T. (2019). *Essential Truths for Principals*. Routledge.

Whitaker, T. (2014). *Shifting the Monkey: The Art of Protecting Good People from Liars, Criers and Other Slackers*. Solution Tree.

7

Being Intentional

I've had many conversations with school leaders over the years about the difference between management and leadership. Linda Carrier (2017) put it like this: "Managers attend to the *checklist of tasks* while leaders also attend to the human dynamic" (34). I've heard the difference framed in a variety of ways, but this is how it has become helpful for me to think about the distinction. Management is about keeping the school operating smoothly. So in a sense it's about maintaining a status quo. Leadership, in contrast, is about moving the organization to a new and greater level. It is about inspiring and empowering those in the organization to achieve the mission to a higher degree. And what is that mission? *Teaching* and *Learning*! That is the core business of our schools. While every principal recognizes the value of teaching and learning, it is important to point out that instructional leadership will not typically happen by accident. It is the result of school leaders being intentional about how they lead and what they prioritize.

"Management" and "Leadership" is not an either/or proposition. In fact, both are essential. Many new teachers find out in their own classroom that passion for teaching doesn't yield good results if there is not good management in place first. Likewise, the entire instructional program does not thrive if the buses don't run on time, if the students don't get fed, if the bathrooms don't work, if student discipline is not enforced, and if the subs don't show up. Principals must ensure their school is managed well. And make no mistake about it, managing a school can bring some headaches. And it's easy to get bogged down in the administrivia of the job. The paper work, the phone calls, the endless emails, and the meetings can be all consuming. Principals are often caught in the grind of running from one crisis to another, putting out fires at every turn, and doing everything they can just to keep the school running and themselves from drowning. In this sort of context, it can be easy to understand how instruction and student learning can take a back seat. I certainly don't want to be dismissive of the many forces demanding the principal's attention, but I hope to make the case that principals can have their cake and eat it too. They can keep the school running and still provide instructional leadership. As noted earlier, however, this balancing act will not happen accidentally. It is the result of principals being deliberate, strategic, and intentional with their choices. And as Whitaker (2020) reminds us, it most definitely is a commitment: "Less effective principals have dozens of reasons for not having time to visit classrooms daily, or at least weekly. Great principals have an equal number of demands placed on their time. They just do not let these reasons keep them from doing what matters most: improving teacher effectiveness in their school" (42). So it's important to look for ways to manage more efficiently (through strategies like delegation) in order to free up some emotional and intellectual bandwidth (not to mention time!) for leading instruction. Instruction needs to be a priority and not an afterthought. Teaching, learning, and student achievement becomes the focus of the school when it is the focus of the principal. DeWitt (2020) reiterates this point in his own writing; "As you can tell from reading this book all of this good advice really comes down to where we put our focus" (104). As the principal, Karissa Lang, put it to me, "What's our goal, what's the pathway to get there, and what are we doing to get there?"

 I'm reminded of an unfortunate autobiographical anecdote at one of my schools, and at the risk of bruising my own "principal ego"—I will share it here. Early in my first year at that school, a teacher cornered me in one of the assistant principal's offices and proceeded to vent about the fact that I didn't care about instruction. She reminded me that at the first faculty meeting of the year, I talked about building relationships with students, cultivating a culture of collaboration, and bringing positive energy to work each day. I didn't talk about teaching, or learning, or rigor, or student achievement. And then she added, "You don't even look at our lesson plans!" She was right about all those things. While I disagreed with her assertion that I didn't care about teaching and learning, I apologized for not communicating it more clearly. And I realized that I had not been as intentional as I should have been about articulating the mission of our school.

What It Looks Like

Communicating the Vision and Mission

The author and motivational speaker, Zig Zigler, quipped, "If you aim at nothing, you'll hit it every time." This poignant adage underscores the importance of having a goal, a destination, or a vision. In a school, articulating that vision is one of the vital roles of the principal. There are copious amounts of research that reinforces this truth. (See the work of Cotton, 2003; and Rouleau, 2021.) Teachers take their cues from the principal. They feed off the energy of the principal. And their sense of focus is shaped by the principal. So principals need to ensure that they are consistently communicating high expectations about the quality of teaching and learning that occurs daily in the classrooms. Smith and Andrews (1989) note, "Communication of vision is perhaps the most important way for a principal to exert effective leadership—to leave no doubt about school priorities" (16). To be fair, most teachers will continue to teach even if the principal never makes it a focus. Teachers are professionals, and teaching is what they do. But a strong vision and a consistent message from the administration can generate high levels of intensity among the faculty and provides the context for the principal to make an impact on teaching and learning. If the vision represents the destination of the school, the mission represents the way it will get there. Every school has a mission statement, and it serves a way of channeling the energy and efforts of the faculty and staff. It provides a strategic focus, and effective principals lead in a way that their actions and priorities are aligned with that focus. Ideally, the mission is not a collection of words in a frame but rather it is a collective pursuit that is woven into the fabric of school life. It is embraced by all the stakeholders. In *The Instructional Leadership Toolbox*, Gupton (2010) provides a word of caution:

> It is more important that the mission be genuine, shared, and well thought out, rather than catchy and easy to recite word for word. Without question however, members of the organization should be able to define easily and in their own words their school's mission, and their individual renditions should vary only in semantics, not in content. (31)

One of the things that I realized several years ago is that I wanted to be predictable as a leader. I began sharing this goal with colleagues. I would ask them what they thought I meant, and we would have a brief conversation about it. I wanted colleagues to understand my rationale for wanting to be predictable. I explained it this way: I want to be so transparent and consistent with my values, that anyone on the staff could predict how I might respond in a given situation. (As an aside, if your staff are consistently blindsided by your decisions, then I suggest some self-reflection. That dynamic would suggest that your colleagues are unclear about what you value or your actions are frequently at odds with your values.)

Bringing it back to instructional leadership, it's crucial that your teachers understand instruction and student achievement is your primary focus. They understand how much you value teaching and learning because that is what drives you. It impacts what you say, what you write, and how you engage with students and staff. Todd Whitaker (2020) underscores the value of being intentional (while also enforcing the benefit of being relational):

> When the principal sneezes, the whole school catches a cold. This is neither good nor bad; it is just the truth.

> Our impact is significant; our focus becomes the school's focus. If we have great credibility and good relationships, people work to please us. If we lack credibility people work against us. Once we make it clear what we want, supporters will work for it and opponents will drag their feet or head the other way. The relations we establish will determine how many are in each camp. We must keep our attention on the issues that matter, not divert our effort and energy to trivial annoyances. (35)

As I spoke with principals preparing for this book, they shared countless examples of ways that they were intentional about a focus on teaching and learning. Daniel Barrentine talked about his "vision planning" beginning as the school year winds down and they move into the summer. He gets feedback from his teachers at the end of the year, and he's able to devote some time to charting the course of the coming school year during the summer when he is not running around the school putting out fires. Their school's high stakes test is administered in March. This past summer they made a plan to administer five practice tests to the students to prepare the students but also to provide formative feedback to teachers during the year. While no school wants their school year to be consumed with standardized tests, this is a clear example of identifying a goal for student achievement, and systematically organizing the year in a way that gives students the best opportunity to be successful.

Annette Sanchez told me that she strives to remind the teachers and students every day why they are here and what she expects. When I asked her how she does that, I was struck by the simplicity and poignancy of her response. Every morning she says over the intercom: "I want kids to learn how to read, to know how to read, and to love to read." She inspired me even more as she continued: "And now I no longer have to say it because I have five-year-olds say it! 'We want to learn how to read. We want to know how to read. And we want to love to read.'"

Ashley Bowling relayed to me that part of their vision relates to the fact that "we are achievers." She said that is a common language they use when talking to students. They frequently use the language of "achievement" in daily interactions. They have been more intentional and strategic with common planning time by asking their teachers to bring a recent assessment to their meetings. That has helped to refocus their collaborative time around teaching and learning. She also highlighted some indirect and perhaps less obvious ways that she was deliberate in shaping the context in which students did their best work. First she has counselors on their instructional leadership team. She acknowledged that it might not be typical, but as she noted: "Mental health matters, so they need to know what we're putting on students instructionally, so they can support us on the back end." She also mentioned to me a practice that I wish I had thought of years ago. Every morning during announcements, she welcomes the subs to the building and tells the students she expects them to treat their substitute teachers with the "Falcon way." Every administrator reading these words can testify to how common it is for the instructional climate to suffer when teachers are out. The practice by this principal represents a deliberate attempt to mitigate that tendency and keep expectations high for student learning.

Owning Your Calendar

I wrote in *Essential Truths for Principals* (Steele & Whitaker, 2019): "It does not matter what you claim to care about; everyone in the building knows what you truly care about by how you spend your time" (37). Leaders cannot afford to be victims of their chaotic circumstances. It's vital that your work calendar reflects your priorities. If someone were to conduct a time audit on your day, what would they discover? Is most of your time spent in your office, in the hallways, in classrooms, in meetings?

I have heard many school leaders over the years talking about writing in time on the calendar to visit classrooms. Typically, what's on the calendar gets done. So the decision to visit classrooms is not made in the moment. For many school leaders, the "moment" in a typical school day is often chaotic and characterized by issues that would most likely fall under the "management and operations" umbrella. It is easy to interpret these issues as urgent, and so they get our attention. When classroom visits are already explicitly on our calendar, we are empowered to put the administrivia on hold.

Far too many times classroom visits are relegated to formal observations, and those are often handled at the last minute and rushed through. Daniel Barrentine has deliberately structured his daily routine that doesn't even require his literal calendar. He'll drop his stuff off in his office in the morning, head to carpool, and then he'll make his rounds, check in on the teachers, and ensure that everyone is focused in the right direction. He knows that if he starts the day in his office, there is a strong chance that he won't get out. He will be pulled in a million directions like every administrator reading this book understands. Jennifer Hogan works in such a large high school, she is pulled in many directions, and there are many things that could trap her in her office. But as she explains, she makes it a priority to maximize the time she does have:

> It's easy when you have 10 or 15 minutes between appointments or you've handled a discipline issue, and then you have a break, and it's easy to stay in your office and catch up on paperwork or check email and do those kind of things, but we really have to capitalize on those small bits of time that we have and not wait for a clearing of our schedule. We have to be intentional about using every time that we can to get out there.

She went on to talk to me about the importance of being intentional with the follow up after visiting a class, whether it's leaving a note, sending a text, shooting an email, or leaving a Vox, saying, "Hey… this is what I saw…"

Being intentional as an instructional leader doesn't always mean visiting classrooms, but it does mean investing your time and energy in activities that have an impact on the success of the instructional program. Alonzo Barkley recognizes that school attendance is foundational to being successful in school. So on a regular basis he reviews an attendance report to see who has excessive absences. He also emails teachers asking them to share names of students who have been missing their class too much.

He'll call parents of those students; he'll text them; he'll meet with them. He will allow students to "buy back" days they missed by attending Saturday School and making up work. He'll also ask teachers to send students to his office who have missed too much class. He says he handles it this way "because I want them to know that I'm paying attention to who was not showing up for their class. I could do it in a lot of ways where they do not even have to worry about it, but I want them to know that this is important to me, that it's important that these kids are in your class learning, and we prioritize learning in your classroom."

Make instruction and learning a priority and a consistent focus for all of your work. Ensure that your staff emails and meeting agendas reflect that priority. Block off time in your calendar to get into classrooms. Ask teachers about their lessons. Talk to students about their experiences in their classes. *Teaching* and *learning* are the core business of the school. Being intentional about how you allocate your time, energy, and resources is a crucial element of your instructional leadership.

Questions for Reflection

Am I clear in my own mind what our instructional and curricular priorities are?

Do the teachers have a clear understanding of the academic focus of the school?

Are the students aware of the academic priorities of the school?

Are parents aware of the academic priorities of the school?

What are the different ways that we communicate our specific focus on teaching and learning?

Are there ways that we can clarify or enhance this messaging?

What are the barriers that prevent me from being more consistent in my articulation of our academic goals?

Are there things in my work that I need to begin saying "no" to that would enable me to be more engaged as the instructional leader of the school?

Am I perceived as the instructional leader of the building? Why or why not?

What are additional strategies we could employ to enhance our vision for teaching and learning?

References

Carrier, L. (2017). *Keeping the Leadership in Instructional Leadership: Developing Your Practice*. Routledge.

Cotton, K. (2003). *Principals and Student Achievement: What the Research Says*. ASCD.

DeWitt, P. (2020). *Instructional Leadership: Creating Practice Out of Theory*. Corwin.

Gupton, S. L. (2010). *The Instructional Leadership Toolbox: A Handbook for Improving Practice*. Corwin.

Rouleau, K. (2021). *Balanced Leadership for Student Learning: A 2021 Update of McREL's Research-Based School Leadership Development Program*. McREL International.

Smith, W. F., & Andrews, R. L. (1989). *Instructional Leadership: How Principals Make a Difference*. ASCD.

Steele, D., & Whitaker, T. (2019). *Essential Truths for Principals*. Routledge.

Whitaker, T. (2020). *What Great Principals Do Differently: 20 Things That Matter Most*. Routledge.

8

Prioritizing Learning, Not Teaching

As a school leader, I am sure that you have amazing teachers in your school. They are creative, inspiring, dynamic, and dedicated. I consider myself fortunate to have had the opportunity to work alongside many great teachers. Teaching is a challenging and stressful profession that carries with it a significant amount of emotional labor. The teachers in our schools deserve our support, our respect, and our unwavering appreciation, and principals should continuously be looking for ways to explicitly communicate how much they value their teachers. As much as we value and honor our teachers, it is important to remember that we do not build and fund schools so teachers will have a place to work. I love teachers. I was one! And I made a career out of working in a school every day. But the purpose of schools, of course, is to ensure students learn. The goal of this chapter is to provide clarity around this goal and reinforce that priority. Amy Fast put it succinctly: "I think every meeting, every professional learning community, every lesson plan, every test… there are two questions that we have to ask ourselves: How are they doing? And how do we know?"

Gupton (2010) argues, "No one dimension of school leadership is more important than a principal's skill and commitment to focusing the school's work on the learner" (104). Because we all know that student learning is the main thing, it becomes easy to take that goal for granted and actually lose sight of the priority. We can spend so much time focusing on the knowledge, skills, and practices of teachers that we actually take our eyes off the ball and forget the fact that learning is where the rubber meets the road. Many years ago, I first heard the adage: "Until something is learned, nothing is taught." That struck me as a profound and somewhat convicting statement. As a teacher, it would be easy to think to myself: "Hey… I taught the material; I can't make the students pay attention, and I certainly can't make them learn!" I understand that sentiment, but ultimately, that is not the type of perspective that defines the most effective educators. As I wrote in *Essential Truths for Teachers* (Steele & Whitaker, 2019): "Great teachers define their success by the success of their students. They understand it's not about the teaching, it's about the learning." I further underscored this point with the following reflection:

> I remember a teacher who would always pester me about when the state test results were coming in. She could not wait to see how her students had done. She spent countless hours tutoring her students and would do anything to help them succeed. She saw the success of her students as a reflection of the work she had done. (38)

Blink (2013) encourages readers to reflect on the following: "Are classroom teachers changing their instruction to meet the needs of students in such a way that it is making a difference in the level of mastery of content? How is that mastery evidenced in the data? What changes need to be made to sustain the effort and to embed it into the everyday instructional practices of the classroom? Are teachers truly becoming educational leaders in their classrooms and taking ownership…?" (9). In a book that had a big impact on my own development as a school leader, Todd Whitaker (2020) writes in *What Great Principals Do Differently*, "Clearly, the best teachers accept responsibility for their classrooms and the worst teachers do not. Effective principles constantly work to make all teachers accept responsibility. More than that, they accept a higher level of responsibility themselves" (20).

What does it mean for the principal to be focused on learning? It means keeping a consistent focus on the evidence that the instructional program is producing the desired results. It means being clear on the desired learning targets or learning outcomes in addition to the metrics used to evaluate the success of those learning goals. DeWitt (2020) puts it succinctly: "instructional leadership is when those in a leadership position focus on implementing practices that will increase student learning" (37). Carrier (2017) also notes, "Instructional leaders communicate that definition of high expectations every day through their verbal and written communications. They possess a clear operational definition of their expectations that is founded upon their mission to be focused on learning" (47). While it seems simple enough to suggest that the goal of teaching is to increase student learning, Glickman et al. (2010, p. 92) underscore the need for true clarity around the instructional goals as they ask us to consider these examples:

- If the goal is for students to master basic skills, then effective teaching might involve explanation, demonstration, practice, feedback, and more practice.
- If the goal is for students to learn classical culture, then effective teaching might consist of reading the great works, lectures, and Socratic discussion.
- If the goal is for students to become problem solvers, then effective teaching might call for exposing students to real-world problems and active student involvement in testing possible solutions and reaching resolutions.
- If the goal is social development, then effective teaching might consist of structuring cooperative learning and community-building activities.

- If the goal is personal development, then effective teaching might mean facilitating the students' self-directed learning and self-assessment.
- If the goal is critical inquiry, then effective teaching might require the teacher to challenge students' current values and assumptions and to ask students to critique dominant belief systems, social structures, and power relationships.

These examples make obvious the notion that specificity around instructional goals is a prerequisite to clarity around instructional practice.

What It Looks Like

Focusing on Evidence

"Data meetings" have become prevalent around the country, and it is for good reason because they provide the opportunity to connect the dots between the instructional goals and the learning outcomes. The data represents the evidence of student learning or lack thereof. In many schools, principals lead data meetings, but that isn't necessarily imperative. Depending on the size of the school, they could be led by an assistant principal, a counselor, a lead teacher, or an instructional coach. What is essential is that you understand what is going on in those meetings, and that your teachers know you value them.

Oftentimes data meetings represent a process for identifying students who are struggling and then recommending academic interventions. This is an important process to be sure, but it should never represent the totality of data analysis within the school. DuFour et al. (2010) wrote extensively about the purpose and structure of professional learning communities (PLCs), and hopefully they are as ubiquitous as data meetings in our schools. Even if they are not called PLCs, it is imperative that groups of teachers meet regularly to review not just instructional practices but the evidence of instructional practices. The results, after all, are what truly matters. Some schools may only have one teacher who teaches a certain grade or subject, so they do not have colleagues to compare results with, but that doesn't mean that they can't reflect on their own results. In *Essential Truths for Teachers* (Steele & Whitaker, 2019), I recounted this story:

> Several years ago, I remember walking into a teacher's room during his planning period. He was finishing up the tests he was grading. He looked a little dejected as he remarked to me: "These students all did poorly. Somehow, I didn't communicate the material as well as I thought I had. I'm gonna reteach it and then assess them again." It can be hard for teachers to swallow their pride in those circumstances, but that is what good teachers are willing to do. They understand the bottom line is always student learning, and ensuring student success is what drives them. (38)

Creating a culture where teachers take this type of ownership in the success of their students is a hallmark of great instructional leadership. When I first joined the Homewood City School System, I noticed that there were some common scripted questions for teacher interviews. There is one that caught my attention: "How do you assess your own effectiveness as a teacher?" Initially, I remember not liking the question because it just seemed a little awkward to me. Eventually, I came to realize how profound it was. It was a question that drove to the core of teaching… learning! We want teachers to measure themselves against the benchmark of student learning. Gupton (2010) advises principals, "Communicate your passion for the success of teachers and students in word and deed" (28). And remember, the success of teachers is always reflected in the success of students. That is the yardstick.

Evaluating Assessment Practices

When you approach the instructional program with this type of an eye toward results, it will inevitably require an evaluation of assessment practices within the school. DuFour et al. (2010) outlined a systematic approach to ensuring instructional effectiveness in *Learning By Doing: A Handbook for Professional Communities at Work*. They posit four central questions:

- What knowledge and skills should every student acquire as a result of this unit of instruction?
- How will we know when they have acquired the central knowledge and skills?
- How will we respond when some students do not learn?
- How will we extend and enrich the learning for students who are already proficient? (28)

These four questions have helped guide administrators and teachers around the world who seek to meet the needs of their students more effectively. The first question is important for developing the curriculum. The third question is important for guiding academic intervention. The fourth question is needed to ensure that we do not have disengaged and bored students. For the purposes of this section, we are focusing on the second question: "How will we know when they have acquired the central knowledge and skills?"

As Amy Fast framed it, "How are they doing, and how do we know?" A word of advice is important here. Please understand that teachers often have deep and longstanding beliefs about their assessment practices. It is no small task to change, or sometimes even tweak, teachers' grading practices. Fast emphasized, "you're changing the rules of the game that everyone's played since they're in kindergarten." She further explained, "Take the time to go fast to go slow. You get people around the table. You have them dive into the research. You have conversations like Socratic seminars as adults to unpack the research together. You talk about the implications and the potential pros and cons of implementing something like this." Rick Wormeli underscored the need for reviewing assessment practices in a recent article for the National Association of Secondary School Principals (2025):

> The "Wild West" nature of grading is troubling. Standardized test scores don't always reflect report card grades. Some teachers count homework as 20% of the

grade while others don't count it at all. Redos and retakes are encouraged in some classes but forbidden in others. Teachers in the same department teaching the same content across different classes record sometimes wildly varying grades for the same level of learning. Some credit recovery programs used for sports eligibility do not hold students accountable for learning course content, yet we consider grades from those programs accurate. Faculty use letter grades, percentages, narrative feedback, 4.0 scale, checks/zeroes, and seven-point rubrics on varying assessments then jam them all into a single, aggregate percentage for a transcript.

Wormeli has written extensively around this topic, and I would strongly recommend him to any school leaders wanting to do a deeper dive with assessment.

The last school that I led took three years to evaluate assessment practices and identify common assessment practices that were consistent with the research and what was best for student learning. They didn't accomplish this in a faculty meeting, an inservice, or a semester of study. They took three years! (For the record, I get no credit for this process; it occurred before I joined the staff.) As you look at assessment practices within your school, these are the sorts of questions worth asking and answering:

- Does our instruction align with our learning targets?
- Do our assessments align with the learning targets?
- Do our assessments reflect mastery of the learning targets?
- Are our homework practices supported by research?
- Do students have multiple attempts to demonstrate mastery?
- Do we believe that students learn at different rates, and do our assessment practices allow for that reality?
- Do any of your teachers have assessment practices that create "grade inflation?"
- What role do our assessment practices play in creating equitable learning experiences for our students?

These are not easy questions to tackle, but they are important nonetheless, for they have the potential to impact the instructional program and the accuracy of how student achievement is communicated to parents and other stakeholders. If you have the courage to lead these conversations with your faculty and the leadership savvy to engage patiently and methodically, you will have made a significant impact on the instructional program of your school and will have taken prodigious strides as an instructional leader.

Examples in the Schools

A focus on student learning can look a lot of different ways. Carmen Maring has conversations with her teachers around grading practices, asking, "Do those essential learning outcomes make sense?" Annette Sanchez focuses on rubrics for student learning in her evaluation conferences, and the teacher does the majority of the talking. Shannon McCaskey talked to me about drilling down on every student, emphasizing that *every* student needs an individualized education plan. She works to keep her teachers focused on academic progress, focusing on the importance of making small strides… "3 or 4 points." Chris Jackson talked about working with teachers on student agency and student-led conferences. He also talked about being intentional with using language that reflected their true focus. For example, when talking about curriculum, they use the term "learning goals" instead of "objectives." He refers to "learning plans" rather than "lesson plans." As he explained to me, "We want to come from the standpoint of focusing on learning, not teaching."

Adam Dovico described to me a story where his teachers were feeling good about their instruction. He actually told me his teachers were "killing it." Teachers were doing creative and fun activities, and the students seemed to be engaged. Teachers from other schools were even coming to tour their school. The faculty's confidence was soaring. And then the standardized test data came in. It was not encouraging. Somehow, there was a disconnect between the engaging instruction and the student learning. Adam had a talented and savvy instructional coach.

She began working with the teachers to break down their lesson plans, the instructional process, and their assessments. What they realized is that in their focus to create "engaging activities" they were inadvertently leaving out chunks of content. They had entertaining and engaging lessons, but the data was not there, so they had to revamp their focus. As he put it, their process was great, but not their product. They realized their engaging process was not effective if it was not accompanied by the product of the desired learning outcomes. Also, please note DoVico's strategic delegation here. Because of the coach's skill, she was able to facilitate this process in a way that some of the teachers were even able to realize the disconnect for themselves. Adam was very quick to give his coach all the credit for this transformative instructional leadership. As discussed in Chapter 6, we need to realize as school leaders that we may have colleagues on our team who can get certain jobs done better than we can.

Alonzo Barkley's school was focused on raising the ACT scores of his Juniors. In his home state, this is a crucial metric for students being admitted into college and receiving scholarship money. They put every 11th grader's name on one side of an index card, and put their pre-ACT score on the other side. They color coded the cards based on whether they were at level one, two, three, or four. As students were able to increase their proficiency, they referred to it as "leveling up." These cards served as a poignant reminder of the academic progress of the students and it facilitated teachers being more mindful of the role they played in contributing to student achievement.

DeWitt (2020) writes, "To me, instructional leadership is not about the leader at all but about how the leader works as a team with their students, staff, and parents to put the focus on learning" (6). So how do you do that in your school? As school leaders, we should always strive to support and reinforce the great work of teachers, but one of the marks of a great instructional leader is that they are able to continually shift the focus of conversations in the school toward student learning. When you're in a classroom, for example, be more preoccupied with the extent to which students are engaged in the lesson than how the teacher is teaching that lesson. In conversations with teachers about their work, always keep student learning and academic progress at the forefront. Create opportunities for teachers to spend time evaluating the evidence of their classroom assessments and standardized tests. Be explicit about communicating the priority of student learning. As a school leader, this is what it means to "keep your eye on the ball."

Questions for Reflection

When I visit classrooms, am I more focused on the teacher or the students?

How do our teachers assess their own effectiveness?

Does our faculty have a shared understanding for what student success looks like?

Do we have a collective understanding of what student engagement looks like, and how it differs from compliance?

Do we know how students perceive their own learning experience, and how those perspectives impact instructional practices in the building?

Do all our students have equitable learning experiences? How do I know that?

How do my communications underscore the goal of student learning?

How do I ensure that our teachers remain mindful of the centrality of student learning?

Are our teachers comfortable sharing their own student performance data?

To what extent is our instructional program driven by high stakes testing, and are we comfortable with the role that it plays?

References

Blink, R. J. (2013). *Data-Driven Instructional Leadership.* Routledge.

Carrier, L. (2017). *Keeping the Leadership in Instructional Leadership: Developing Your Practice.* Routledge.

DeWitt, P. (2020). *Instructional Leadership: Creating Practice Out of Theory.* Corwin.

DuFour, R., DuFour, R., Eaker, R., & Many, T. (2010). *Learning by Doing: A Handbook for Professional Learning Communities at Work.* Solution Tree Press.

Glickman, C., Gordon, S., & Ross-Gordon, J. (2010). *Supervision and Instructional Leadership: A Developmental Approach.* Pearson.

Gupton, S. L. (2010). *The Instructional Leadership Toolbox: A Handbook for Improving Practice.* Corwin.

Steele, D., & Whitaker, T. (2019). *Essential Truths for Teachers.* Routledge.

Whitaker, T. (2020). *What Great Principals Do Differently: 20 Things That Matter Most.* Routledge.

Wormeli, R. (2025, May). When Our Grading Philosophies Conflict with Those of Our Faculties. A Principal Leadership Article in Viewpoint. *NASSP.* www.nassp.org/publication/principal-leadership/volume-25-2024-2025/principal-leadership-may-2025/viewpoint-may-2025

9

Removing Barriers

In the fall of 2011, I was only a few weeks into my first principalship. I noticed that I was copied on an exchange of emails between one of my veteran teachers and a frustrated parent. As I recall, there had been a testy exchange between the teacher and this lady's son as they were entering the school building in the morning. The mother felt like her son was being harassed over a period of several days, and the teacher was aggravated that her son was not following procedures and had become disrespectful. The mother was in "mama bear" mode, and the teacher was feeling under attack. After several days of tense back and forth emails, we had a parent conference in my office with the teacher and the parent. To be honest, I don't remember all the details of that conference. Having been an assistant principal for ten years, I had handled too many parent conferences to count. I generally felt comfortable and confident in those meetings. My approach is always to work diplomatically toward resolution and hopefully achieve a win/win result. This particular conference was no different in that regard. We had the conference, and I didn't give it another thought. As it turns out, my veteran teacher did. As I was starting our next faculty meeting, I was caught off guard when this teacher jumped up, walked to the front of the library and asked if she could take over for a minute. She then shared a few words with the faculty that went something like this: "Y'all, I will admit that I did not have high hopes for our young new principal when I first met him in May. With his baby face, and lack of prior principal experience, I just knew parents would walk all over him. But let me tell you, I had an issue with a mom last week, and at that parent conference, he shut that mom down! I was so impressed with his strong support, I would like to honor him with the 'Baby Face Nelson' award. He might look young, but he's tough like a gangster."

She even gave me a framed certificate which commemorated this unique honor. This was obviously a career highlight for me. I had learned as a young assistant principal that administrators are defined by their ability to support their teachers. It is an insight that I have shared many times over the years as I have had the opportunity to mentor young administrators. It was tremendously gratifying to me to know that this teacher felt so supported by me in that conference.

So what does this story have to do with instructional leadership? In *The 21 Irrefutable Laws of Leadership* (2007), John Maxwell wrote, "Leadership is about influence—nothing more, nothing less" (16). So instructional leadership is about having influence on teaching and learning. When my teacher was reading those long emails from the mother, she was not focused on her teaching. When she was venting to a colleague about having to deal with an "irrational parent," she was not planning lessons. Every time the parent got under her skin, she probably lost a little bit of energy. The challenge of engaging with that parent was a sort of hurdle for her at work. It represented a barrier in her job. So when I was able to help her with that parent, I actually helped make it possible for her to focus her time and energy where it should be—her students.

I think school leaders have in their head a list of actions or activities that they would lump under the umbrella of instructional leadership. Leading data meetings, observing teachers and providing feedback, facilitating professional development, talking about brain research, and participating in professional learning communities are all stereotypical examples of what most administrators would call instructional leadership. As I alluded to in the introduction, it is my goal in writing this book to encourage school leaders to reconceptualize their notion of instructional leadership and recognize that the umbrella is actually bigger than they might have realized. Our influence over teaching and learning is not limited to those stereotypical activities. I hope for the reader to connect the dots, for example, from helping a teacher navigate a tough parent conference to contributing to her ability to devote more time to her teaching.

What It Looks Like

I've heard it said many times that leaders should "hire great people and then get out of their way." There is a lot of truth to that, but I suggest that we consider a twist to that quip. "Hire great people, and commit yourself to removing obstacles that are *in* their way and providing the resources that they need to do their job well."

Teachers talk about the joy of "light bulb moments" in their classroom. It is when kids get a spark in their eye that reveals they just understood a concept. These moments are enormously gratifying for teachers and serve as powerful reminders that they chose the right profession. Because administrators don't usually get to teach students, they don't get to have these same rewarding experiences. It was something of an epiphany for me as an assistant principal when I recognized the need to redefine *my* light bulb moments. As an administrator, my rewarding moments were when I could help a teacher… when I could help them move a desk, support them with a disruptive student, collaborate with them to write a dicey email, have their back in a parent conference. These were the moments that made me feel like I was adding value. These became moments that I relished.

When you lead through relationships, it is not too difficult to discover ways that you can support your teachers. When you listen to your teachers they are often eager to share ways you can support them… challenges with which they need help… or resources that would be game changers in their classroom. Shannon McCaskey talked to me about advocating for her teachers to the district office. Her school was a high poverty school, and her teachers dealt with unique challenges that frequently characterize Title I schools. The lack of resources was having a negative impact on student learning. She also told me that her teachers were having to give too many mandated assessments, and they were pulled away from the classroom too often for professional development. These were also issues she raised at the district level. Through advocating to her superiors, she ingratiated herself to her teachers and she positively impacted the instructional program. Another principal told me a story of his experience with diplomatically pushing back against the district office as they were requiring the implementation of a certain initiative that was not working in his school. It goes without saying that principals need to exercise tact and political savvy when navigating those waters, but his account struck me as a poignant example of a school leader advocating for the best interest of his teachers, his students, and the instructional program. Peter DeWitt wrote about the importance of having the courage to make one's voice heard in his book on instructional leadership (2020):

> Leadership is about going against the grain and using your voice to speak up about the things that you believe are harmful to learning. If you are against high-stakes testing, say so. If you think high-stakes testing is necessary, then say that. Leadership is about using your voice, even if it means going up against others. It is hard, but it is very, very worth it. (3)

As I was working on this book, I zoomed with a former superintendent named Kenny Southwick who now leads a co-op of 35 school districts in the Kansas City area. He is about to begin his fiftieth year in education, and I was mesmerized listening to the leadership lessons he had learned over the years. The fact that he still demonstrated genuine passion and commitment for this work struck me as truly inspiring. He reminded me of the importance of relational leadership when he used the phrase, "lead with disposition, not position." And when he talked about the need to support teachers, I assured him that his words would end up in my book. As he talked about the myriad of pressures and responsibilities pressing down upon teachers and the range of initiatives that pull at that their time and energy, he introduced me to the phrase "strategic abandonment." He stressed the need for school leaders to reflect on and evaluate the things we are asking of teachers and to have the courage to let go of the things that don't add value. There are times when we even need to take the bold step of taking something good off the plate. It's imperative that we recognize that our teachers have finite amounts of time and energy that can be reasonably expended on work while retaining a healthy work/life balance, and we should prioritize our efforts accordingly.

Eliminating Friction

My last superintendent would lead his leadership team (which included us principals) through a different book study every year. My final year with the district, we read the book *Fans First* (2022) by Jesse Cole. Cole is the owner and driving force behind the wildly successful exhibition baseball team the Savannah Bananas. After the previous team, the Savannah Sand Gnats, relocated to Columbia, SC, Cole was charged with the creation of a new team. After a public "name the team" contest, the Savannah Bananas were born. *Fans First* is the story of how the transformation and rebranding of a baseball team unfolded. The title of the book stems from Cole's conviction (and one he pursued relentlessly) that the team's fans should always be the focus of every decision. For our purposes here, consider "fans" to be your teachers. (I understand the students are our most important stakeholders, but I've learned over the years that when school leaders take care of the teachers, the teachers are able to take care of their students more effectively.)

One of the chapters in *Fans First* that resonated with me was called "Eliminate Friction," and it serves as a useful way to think about the strategy advocated in this current chapter. Cole explains, "Eliminating friction is about putting yourself in your fans' shoes and looking at every possible pain point, every possible frustration, every possible policy that slows things down, heats up tempers, and punishes fans" (85). Remember school leaders… when you read "fans," think teachers! The first example he describes involves a promotion that the team ran that involved a family meal from Chick-fil-A, game tickets, and team hats. Cole recalled seeing a family approach the entrance, but then promptly get in the car and leave when they encountered the policy that didn't allow outside food inside the stadium. Cole changed that policy because it was counterproductive to their overall goal of winning over fans. Another policy change involved the implementation of all-you-can-eat free concessions. Their upfront ticket price was higher than other teams, and that proved to be a win with fans who felt frustrated at the game being "nickeled and dimed" for every little thing. An example of what Cole called a "microfriction"—a smaller, perhaps even unnoticed annoyance—involved the fact that fans had a hard time contacting the front office because the phone number was so hard to find. They alleviated that hassle by featuring the phone number so prominently on their website that it was impossible not to notice. Cole and his team worked relentlessly to identify and eliminate anything that aggravated, annoyed, or interfered with the fan experience. Cole enjoins his readers to remember: "eliminating friction isn't passive. It should be part of your day-to-day processes" (86).

So consider points of friction for your teachers. Maybe the process for obtaining purchase orders is cumbersome and could be streamlined. Maybe the staff bathroom frequently runs out of toilet paper and the soap dispenser is broken. Maybe teachers have to go out of their way to heat up their lunch because there is no microwave in the lunchroom. Maybe you have a teacher who is being worn out by one "high maintenance" parent. (I actually intervened in one situation and told the parent she could no longer email the teacher. She would need to go through me with any concerns. This teacher was feeling beaten down by this parent, and the reading and responding to so many frivolous emails was taking time away from his other responsibilities.) Perhaps the specific requirements for lesson plans is a point of friction. I know that reasonable people can disagree on the need for teachers to submit lesson plans, but surely we can work to minimize unnecessary hassles connected to it. By the way, the principal who led the highest achieving school I ever worked at did not require lesson plans. I asked him one time what he would do if he became aware of a teacher who was not demonstrating effective planning or organization with their lessons. He responded that he would require lesson plans from *that* teacher. I realize this uniquely individualized approach might not be feasible in states with strong unions, but that still struck me as a compelling example of differentiated leadership.

Perhaps the most salient source of friction for teachers involves the management of disruptive student behavior. If you are the only administrator in your building, or if you are an assistant principal, there is a good chance that student disciplinary referrals consume huge portions of your day. It is easy to view this time as tedious, mundane, and an obstacle to you engaging in "real instructional leadership." I encourage you to consider time spent with challenging students differently. Cotton (2003) notes:

> From the earliest research to the present day, the principal's establishment and maintenance of a safe, orderly school environment has been identified as the most fundamental element of effectiveness. Effective principals bring about this kind of environment by exhibiting personal warmth and accessibility, ensuring that there is broad-based agreement about standards for student behavior, communicating high behavioral standards to students, seeking input from students about behavior policies, applying rules consistently from day to day and from student to student, delegating disciplinary authority to teachers, and providing in-school suspension accompanied by support for seriously disruptive students. (8)

The time you spend handling student discipline actually represents your commitment to ensuring teachers can teach without disruption. That matters! It is time well spent in protecting the instructional program.

One of my enduring memories from my last year as principal involved copy machines. I'm sure many readers can commiserate. Our machines were jamming so frequently and in ways that teachers could not easily troubleshoot that it actually started to affect staff morale. As a principal, I don't typically think about copiers, and our secretary would usually handle the service calls when they were needed. But this was becoming a big deal. I invited one of my teacher leaders to text me when there was another issue. I met in person with the service managers, and one of them began texting me to see how things were going. Things started to improve. Fighting with copy machines had been a significant hassle for teachers; it delayed them being prepared for class; it interfered with them having the materials they needed for their students, and it wasted their time. I fought for my teachers to have what they needed, and I certainly wanted them to know I cared about this ridiculous friction in their job.

Pay close attention to the work of your teachers, and frequently put yourself in their shoes. Talk to them about what their challenges are, about what the stress points are in their job. And really listen! But then please don't respond by saying: "I know that's hard. I'm proud of your resilience. Thanks for the great work." Actually work to provide solutions however you can. The poet and artist known as Vanilla Ice once claimed: "If there's a problem… yo, I'll solve it." That's a great attitude for instructional leaders! Identify problems that confront your staff and work to solve them when you can. You would be amazed at how some little interventions on behalf of your teachers will go a long way.

Providing Resources

Be aware that providing resources is another way to remove barriers and to support the work of your teachers. Cotton's (2003) review of the research led her to write, "Effective principals were creative in finding ways to secure resources necessary to make professional development opportunities available. In fact, principals of high-achieving schools are adept at finding and providing resources—financial, human, time, materials, and facilities—for all kinds of instruction-related needs" (36).

Ashley Bowling had a history department that was conscientious but frustrated with the lack of updated standards from the state. The teachers wanted a clearer and more coherent focus with how they approached their content, so she worked with them to explore and develop a new curriculum. A high school principal recounted the story of a second year teacher who showed potential but demonstrated glaring deficiencies in other ways. The next school year, she placed one of her superstar special education inclusion teachers in that classroom to serve as an informal mentor and role model. Neither the young teacher nor the inclusion teacher knew about the principal's strategy, but it worked beautifully. The principal had the confidence in her veteran special education teacher that she would have a positive impact on the general education teacher just by doing her job like she typically did.

At one of my schools, our three sixth grade math teachers did research and attended some training on interactive smart panels. These are ubiquitous in many schools now, but they were not at the time my teachers came to me requesting this resource. I was able to work with my bookkeeper and pool different funds from various accounts and purchase these panels. They were installed and became game changers in our math classrooms. My teachers were profoundly grateful. Blink (2013) notes:

> Regardless of the abilities of the children in front of a teacher in any given year, those students have to perform, and it is up to the teacher to make that happen. It is the responsibility of school district leaders to provide teachers with every possible tool to assist them and their students on their journey toward success. (66)

Teachers do the core work of the school. If you can take something off their plate… if you can find a resource they need… if you can help them solve a problem… if you collaborate with them to work through a tricky situation—all of this support in the classroom and around the school allows them to spend more time and energy on meeting the needs of their students. Make it a priority to provide teachers what they need to be effective and work to minimize whatever distracts from their primary responsibility… teaching their students.

Questions for Reflection

What are the points of friction that would bother you if you were still in the classroom?

Who are the teachers on your staff that will let you know the friction points?

Are there points of friction in your school that you feel powerless to address? Why is that? And how might you collaborate with colleagues in your district to think outside the box and make a difference for your faculty?

Do you have a formal mechanism for staff members to report issues of concern?

Are there redundancies in required paperwork, or are there paperwork requirements that can be streamlined?

Is there anything on your teachers' plates that you might be able to remove?

Do your teachers feel comfortable asking you for assistance with challenging parents?

Are you aware of the resources that are on the "wish list" of teachers, and what are the ways you might explore obtaining funds to purchase needed resources.

Do you have colleagues at the district level who may be inadvertently creating friction or stress for your teachers, and what are diplomatic or strategic ways that you might "run interference" on behalf of your faculty?

References

Blink, R. J. (2013). *Data-Driven Instructional Leadership*. Routledge.

Cole, J. (2022). *Fans First*. Lioncrest.

Cotton, K. (2003). *Principals and Student Achievement: What the Research Says*. ASCD.

DeWitt, P. (2020). *Instructional Leadership: Creating Practice Out of Theory*. Corwin.

Maxwell, J. (2007). *The 21 Irrefutable Laws of Leadership*. Thomas Nelson.

10

Focusing on the Culture

Countless books have been written about school culture. It is an area for research and study totally unto itself. Gupton (2010, p. 45) describes it as "that nebulous, illusive, invisible, but utterly pervasive and powerful school quality." So why would a book on instructional leadership include a chapter on culture? My own experience, intuitions, and research over the years have validated the direct connection between culture, teaching, and student achievement, and every principal I spoke with in preparing for this book reinforced the crucial link between a school's culture and the effectiveness of the instructional program. Furthermore, decades of research have underscored the link between school culture and student achievement as illustrated in the report of Cotton (2003) as well as the Balanced Leadership Framework described by Rouleau (2021). Many of the school leaders I interviewed even said it was the most important factor in student achievement. To put it bluntly, teaching and learning does not happen in a vacuum. They happen in a context… or a *culture* that supports teaching and learning. Teachers and students thrive when the culture of the school is strong. In the following pages, I will highlight some of the key elements of a school's culture—what Gupton (2010) also described as a school's "organizational superglue"—and I'll provide examples of how that looks in various schools. While there are many different ways one could describe the essential elements of a school's culture, I'm choosing to focus on the following five areas:

- A Culture Focused on Students
- A Culture of Trust
- A Culture of High Expectations
- A Culture of Collaboration
- A Culture of Good Energy

What It Looks Like

A Culture Focused on Students

Glickman et al. (2010) wrote the defining textbook on instructional leadership—one that was often cited here in my own book. But their text, replete with research, theory, and jargon, contained a poignant caveat in the conclusion. They explained their book "is first and foremost about the ideas of purpose, hope, and growth and the development of all our students" (476). This is the sentiment and ambition that should pervade all our schools. I begin this chapter with a discussion of a focus on students because it reinforces our ultimate purpose. The students are why we come to work. Ensuring that the school is focused on the wellbeing of students is foundational to everything else we do.

Unfortunately, there are times when adults can lose their "true north." They can lose sight of the primacy of positive relationships with students. One principal described to me how when she first came to the school, "the culture and the climate was just off." She said that most of the teachers were doing the absolute minimum, and there seemed to be little commitment to developing a school where kids love coming. There was not good collegiality as she noted that some of the adults didn't even speak to one another. She knew things needed to change. For her, it started with the way she engaged with students as she walked down the hall. She called them by name, and interacted with them the way she interacted with parents. She would confront teachers who yelled at their students or engaged in less than respectful tones. Not everyone was on board with the new approach, and the change didn't happen overnight… but it did happen. And she stressed that one of her missions became hiring teachers who loved coming to work, were passionate about students and were committed to creating a positive school environment in which they could thrive. When I asked a former colleague of mine about the significance of culture, she immediately talked about the importance of showing respect to students and taking a genuine interest in them. She's learned students are more likely to be willing to engage when they have a teacher who cares about them as individuals. We all have memories of working with students who are discouraged or have some type of drama that is distracting them. As Kafele (2025) noted, "The environment outside the school walls matters and affects learning on multiple levels" (22). When teachers take the time to talk to students and provide an outlet, it increases their potential for focusing on the instruction at hand.

It would seem intuitively obvious that student engagement is closely correlated with student learning. It seems equally obvious that lesson quality is a crucial factor that influences student engagement. But the principal Jon Wennstrom explained to me that it is not the only factor—as he explained, "When students feel more connected to their teachers they're more engaged. They are more involved. They take the tasks more seriously." So as teachers build personal connections with their students, they create a culture in their classroom where students are more likely to persevere in academic challenges and strive to meet the high bar set by their teacher. Wennstrom also noted that their classrooms spend 25 minutes a day in "community building." This district-wide initiative clearly represents a commitment to cultivating classroom environments that foster high student achievement.

While I was zooming with Alonzo Barkley, I asked him if there was another way that he could frame his efforts about being intentional to keep the mission and vision of the school before the teachers. I was not prepared for his response. He grabbed a two inch replica diamond off his desk, and told me he gave one to every staff member—custodians, CNP workers, office workers, everyone. He explained to his colleagues that the diamond represented the beauty and value of each of their students. He talked about seeing the best in the students, focusing on potential rather than flaws. His account became even more powerful when he took a baggie out of his desk drawer that contained lumps of coal. He rubbed the coal around in his hands, and they became visibly dirty. He would demonstrate this for the teachers and challenged them to focus on the beautiful diamond rather than the nasty coal, challenging them to "make human connections with your kids because that's how you're gonna win them over and draw them in." Kafele describes the need for a "surplus-mindset teacher who sees the greatness in every child that they encounter, even when the child doesn't see greatness in oneself or exhibit greatness in real time" (2025, p. 63).

During the course of my administrative career, I have tried a number of things to try to keep our teachers focused on students. As a young assistant principal, my office was often a revolving door of students with discipline referrals. I reached a point where I decided I wanted to be more than a dispenser of consequences. I wanted to be continually mindful of the important work we are engaged in as we connect with students on a daily basis. I thought about the tradition of athletic teams touching inspirational signs in their locker rooms, and I hoped to apply that ritual or tradition to my office and our school. I emailed our teachers, asking them what they thought should be on a sign that students touched after they left my office. I decided on this message: I AM THE DIFFERENCE! I further described the impact of this sign in *The Total Teacher* (2022):

> Our carpentry class made the sign, and I hung it over my door. Over the years I tried to cultivate a tradition of students touching the sign. To me, this was the ultimate message of empowerment for our students. It is a message that communicates to students that they do not need to be victims of their circumstances. I wanted our students to understand that their behavior and their attitude was the determining factor—whatever the situation might be. I also liked our teachers to touch the sign. I wanted them to

be reminded of the pivotal role that *they* play. *They* are the difference in their classroom. *They* are the difference in our school. *They* are the difference for our students! One year, I gave out bracelets to our staff members that said: "I am the difference!" At one faculty meeting, we even had it written on a cookie cake. This was a theme that I continually emphasized with our faculty. I never wanted our teachers to forget about the potential they had to be difference-makers for their students. (64)

At one of my schools, we also created a "Wall of Dreams." It was homemade from two 4' × 8' white shower boards that our maintenance technician secured together and fastened to the wall in one of our main hallways. We asked all 500 of our sixth graders to write their dream on the wall. These were some of the poignant dreams that our 11-year-olds wrote, also relayed in *The Total Teacher* (Steele, 2022):

> "I want to get better at math."
> "My dream is to be a loving mother."
> "My dream is for my sister to get out of the Air Force alive."
> "I want to do something that MEANS something."
> "My dream is to go to Paris, go to UAB, and get my first kiss."
> "I want the world to hear my voice."
> "I wish my dad would get out of jail." (65)

Certainly we want to see our students achieve academically. But this wall of dreams served to keep us focused on the individual and unique nature of the young lives we were teaching. Our students have passions, desires, and struggles that the adults in the building often know little about, and this was a powerful testament to that reality. It was a daily reminder about the importance of our work, and the individuals with whom we are working.

A Culture of Trust

What does it mean for there to be a culture of trust in the school building? It is sometimes easier to understand a dynamic by describing what it is *not*. A faculty that does not enjoy a culture of trust is often characterized by a mindset of "us against them"—*us* being the teachers and *them* being the administration. Sometimes the lack of trust is reflected in the fractured relationships among teachers. Both dynamics are toxic and undermine any potential for constructive collaboration within the building. Gupton writes:

> Wholesome school communities are built on a culture of mutual trust and respect among members—students, classified staff, teachers, administrators, parents, and community members. This paves the way for internal harmony, cooperation, and smooth functioning which enable the best instructions and learning to take place. (53)

While there is not one clear prescription for how to cultivate this type of culture, it begins with a commitment from staff members to giving their colleagues the benefit of the doubt. The school leader should be constantly looking for ways to reinforce common values and aspirations, and highlighting mutually shared goals. Patrick Lencioni's landmark leadership book *The Five Dysfunctions of a Team* (2002) is a great resource for leaders desiring to more effectively understand and address a culture of distrust.

I spoke with one superintendent who had recently moved from the role of principal to superintendent. In many ways she assumed leadership in a district that was underperforming and in need of state assistance; it was dysfunctional in a variety of ways. She was the sixth superintendent in six years. There were low expectations for students and for staff. When we spoke, she was halfway through her second year in this new role. She indicated that she had to fire six people in the first year because of intentional undermining of colleagues or the organization, but she also recognized that culture is not entirely a function of staffing, as she quipped: "You're never going to fire your way to instructional greatness." She was leading a school district where staff members were primarily concerned with their own wellbeing, not that of the district. In that type of culture, it is not uncommon to stab colleagues in the back or throw them under the bus. She quickly recognized that building a culture of trust and teamwork was a prerequisite to spending energy on teaching and learning. So in the first year, she said, "Literally everything we did is focus on teamwork. It sounds really basic, but it's working as a functional team. It requires leaning into healthy conflict and not sweeping issues under the rug. It means holding each other accountable and not just telling on someone to a superior or doing something to undermine someone." It is incumbent upon school leaders to acknowledge the importance of healthy relationships between the adults in the school and to be proactive about cultivating a culture of trust when it is not evident. Effective instructional leadership is predicated in part by a spirit of goodwill and mutual respect among the adults, and very little progress in the instructional program will be made without it.

A Culture of High Expectations

It can be tempting to view school culture exclusively through the lens of the quality of relationships in the building… teacher-to-teacher, teacher-to-student, and student-to-student. But Cas McWaters underscored to me the concept of a "culture of excellence." For him, that was about the high expectations that were maintained for everyone in the school. A school culture that is built on valuing and respecting students is a great start, but it doesn't end there. Cotton (2003) writes:

> The principal's expression of high expectations for students is part of the vision that guides high-achieving schools and is a critical component in its own right. Researchers… have consistently found that high achieving schools (including poor and minority schools) are successful in part because the principals communicate to everyone in the school their expectations of high performance. (11–12)

This culture of high expectations is not just something that strong principals try to cultivate amongst the students and staff, it is something that they model themselves, as highlighted by Whitaker (2020): "All principals—including our most effective and our least effective colleagues—have high expectations for their teachers. The difference between average and great principals lies in *what they expect of themselves*" (17).

Alonzo Barkley worked hard to inspire his teachers about the difference they make with students, but he didn't stop with just trying to motivate teachers. He wanted to set the bar high for his students. He told me their school had seen a lot of success developing great musicians and great athletes, but it was vital that they "start to create great academic students." One example of their attempt to value academic achievement was a group called the "25 club." They devoted a wall in the school to spotlighting pictures of students who had scored a 25 or higher on the ACT. They also raised expectations for student attendance with their systematic tracking of student absences, which was discussed in Chapter 7.

Daniel Barrentine began leading a high school that was experiencing significant challenges with student discipline. He found that he could get the staff more on board with the type of culture he desired for the school "if we created an expectation for our students first." The administration became focused on enforcing higher standards for student behavior with increased accountability and what he called "tough love." Barrenine described that they were able to win over many of their teachers as they witnessed the new standard upheld for students. These teachers became much more amenable to his other ideas on school culture. Adam Dovico also talked to me about inheriting a school without a strong culture, in part because of poor student behavior. Like Barrentine, Dovico also discovered that as he was proactive with addressing student behavioral issues, the culture improved, and he earned the credibility with teachers to engage with them on issues around instruction.

A Culture of Collaboration

We talked in Chapter 6 about the critical need for school leaders to collaborate with teachers in the leading and operating of the school. The value of a collaborative culture is supported by the research that is described here by Cotton (2003):

> Closely related to the benefits of shared decision making are the researchers' discoveries about the positive outcomes that emerge when principals and others establish and maintain a truly collaborative culture. In such a culture, … there is a norm of principal, teachers, and others learning and planning and working together to upgrade their skills and knowledge and improve their school. (23)

It is important to note that just as teaching and learning does not happen in a vacuum, neither does collaboration among the adults. It occurs in schools where there is mutual respect among colleagues, and teachers understand that the students benefit when the adults in the building work well together. Sometimes teachers are friends with each other outside of school. They might go out for drinks after work, or hang out together on the weekend. While it can be a nice perk to have such camaraderie with your colleagues; it's not necessary. What is necessary is that teachers collaborate professionally. This means they communicate well with each other, collaborate to plan lessons, develop assessments, coordinate academic interventions, and collectively brainstorm strategies to meet the unique needs of shared students. Building a culture of collaboration is not always easy, though, as DeWitt (2020) explains:

> As you may have guessed, getting adults to come together and focus on a goal is not an easy task. Many of us, in the field of education, entered into the teaching profession because we loved working with children and young adults or we loved specific content. Perhaps we had great experiences in school as students that we wanted to continue as teachers. Or we had negative experiences in school that we wanted to prevent for the next generation of students. My point is that while most of us share a passion either for teaching children or for a

particular subject, we did not enter the field of teaching with other adults. Working with adults can be challenging and frustrating. We are so used to controlling our domains as teachers that it's hard to let go of that control when working with other adults. (100)

In healthy schools, the adults share mutual respect, but they also value the contributions of their colleagues. There is an old adage: "The whole is stronger than the sum of its parts." Great instructional leaders recognize this wisdom, and they work to apply that insight to their school. They are always looking for ways to create opportunities for adults to work together, and they are validating that collaboration at every opportunity. The bottom line is that students benefit when the adults work together on their behalf. Effective instructional leadership includes creating a culture that encourages, leverages, and celebrates collaboration among the faculty.

A Culture of Good Energy

"The way you feel when you come to work has an effect on the way you teach." As we connect the dots between culture and student learning, it is hard to imagine a more poignant explanation than this comment from Annette Sanchez. When teachers enjoy coming to work, when they enjoy their job, they are typically more effective. And the attitude of the teachers obviously trickles down to the experience of the students. In my own experience, students are aware of the mood of their teachers. Students can sense when their teachers enjoy teaching, and they can sense when it appears to be drudgery. The attitude of the teacher has an impact on the attitude of the students, and the attitude of the students has an impact on their approach to the lesson. One teacher described to me a colleague who seemed to be in a bad mood every day and whose daily demeanor had a profoundly negative impact on the climate of the classroom and on the attitude of the students. You can imagine the poor quality of learning experiences in that class. There is not one formula for how school leaders can build a school culture where teachers enjoy teaching and students enjoy learning. There is not a silver bullet or magic pill for building a positive school environment. But please know that the learning environment matters.

It is foolish for teachers to ignore these outside influences or to assume students can pretend that their drama isn't real. Just as students bring "baggage" into the school, the adults do as well. School leaders should be mindful of this reality. While I am touting the value of bringing good energy to work, I am not advocating what some cynics would label "toxic positivity." I am not encouraging educators to be "Pollyanna," or to bury their heads in the sand, or to be in denial about real adversity that may exist. In fact, it is imperative that school leaders give their teachers the freedom to be human. They need to extend the grace to their teachers to experience the normal range of emotions like frustration, discouragement, anxiety, and depression. Teachers do amazing work with students, and over my career I was often in awe of their creativity, their compassion, their dedication, and their resilience. These qualities are remarkable to be sure, but they do not make teachers superheroes. They are ordinary people who achieve remarkable results with the students under their care. I believe that when school leaders make allowance for the human frailty of their colleagues and extend grace in the challenging times, it goes a long way toward elevating staff morale and fostering the type of culture that is characterized by positive energy. Remember the adage, "employees don't leave jobs; they leave bosses." This sentiment speaks to the importance of school leaders consistently showing patience, understanding, and empathy toward their teachers. Principals cannot change the challenging circumstances that confront many of their teachers both inside and outside of school. They actually are continuously tasked with navigating their *own* drama and adversity. But they can choose to model what it means to be resilient, optimistic, and hopeful in the midst of it all. Leading by example helps to foster the sort of culture that inspires and empowers the teachers in the school to follow suit.

How do school leaders generate good energy in the building? To start with, the qualities outlined in previous chapters go a long way toward this end. Teachers appreciate it when their administration is supportive. They appreciate it when their administration is visible. They appreciate it when their professional expertise is recognized and valued. They appreciate it when they are included in the decision-making process. They appreciate it when their administration removes barriers and is gracious with providing resources. They appreciate it when the administration removes points of friction. As a father of two sons and a daughter who all played basketball when they were young, I talked to them a lot about the importance of "keeping your head on a swivel." At various times, they all played point guard which is the position tasked with bringing the ball up the court and making good passes to run the offense. I would say things like: "Alright, keep your head up, always scanning the court, keeping your head on a swivel, always looking for the open teammate and the most effective pass." Great principals keep their head on a swivel, always looking for ways to support their staff, take something off their plate, or to make their load a little lighter. Teachers appreciate working for leaders like that. They notice all of the kind words and supportive gestures, and I would suggest it impacts both their job satisfaction and their job performance.

Some final thoughts on strategies for cultivating positive energy in the school: Celebrate successes of both teachers and students. Make a point of having fun at work… and sometimes even being silly. Create unique traditions. Play practical jokes on colleagues. Look for opportunities to play music, either in the hall or during morning announcements. Finally, don't take yourself too seriously.

While doing these things might not seem like you're engaged in "instructional leadership," it will create an environment where teachers and students do their best work. And that's the goal.

Questions for Reflection

How would students, parents, and staff describe the culture of our school?

What are the elements of school culture that support teaching and learning?

What are additional ways that our school could center our culture on the needs and wellbeing of students?

How do I communicate high expectations to the students and staff?

What are additional ways that we can foster and reinforce collaboration among teachers?

What are ways that I show our teachers that I care about them as individuals?

How do I model resilience? Optimism? Hope?

What are the ways that I gauge staff morale throughout the school year?

What are the things about our school culture that give me heartburn?

What are ways to elevate the energy of the school that we have not yet tried?

References

Cotton, K. (2003). *Principals and Student Achievement: What the Research Says*. ASCD.

DeWitt, P. (2020). *Instructional Leadership: Creating Practice out of Theory*. Corwin.

Glickman, C., Gordon, S., & Ross-Gordon, J. (2010). *Supervision and Instructional Leadership: A Developmental Approach*. Pearson.

Gupton, S. L. (2010). *The Instructional Leadership Toolbox: A Handbook for Improving Practice*. Corwin.

Kafele, B. (2025). *What Is My Value Instructionally to the Teachers I Supervise?* ASCD.

Lencioni, P. (2002). *The Five Dysfunctions of a Team: A Leadership Fable*. Jossey-Bass.

Rouleau, K. (2021). *Balanced Leadership for Student Learning: A 2021 Update of McREL's Research-Based School Leadership Development Program*. McREL International.

Steele, D. (2022). *The Total Teacher: Understanding the Three Dimensions that Define Effective Educators*. Routledge.

Whitaker, T. (2020). *What Great Principals Do Differently: 20 Things That Matter Most*. Routledge.

Conclusion

Many of the qualities, dispositions, and commitments discussed in this book are inextricably interconnected. I had trouble deciding, for example, whether I included my discussion on the Johari Window in the chapter on *vulnerability* or the chapter on being *relational*. I could have even included it in the chapter on being *curious* because it reflects the importance of caring about and then coming to terms with the various ways that you are perceived by others. The attributes outlined in the previous pages work to complement each other and frequently reinforce each other. A measure of *vulnerability* is inherent in *curiosity*. Meaningful *reflection* with teachers is only possible in the context of *relational* trust. A *focus on student learning* is predicated on strategic *intentionality*. There are countless examples of ways that they cross over in the work of a principal and in the life of a principal. Here are just a few:

> Being *vulnerable* and being *visible* goes a long way to increase your capacity for being *relational*.
> Being *curious* is in itself an example of being *vulnerable*—as it's a tacit admission that you don't know everything.
> Being *focused on student learning* represents a great example of being *intentional*.
> Being *visible* provides great opportunities to *remove barriers* or points of friction.
> Being *relational* is a fantastic way to *build a culture* that prioritizes human connections within the building. Being *relational* also increases the likelihood that teachers will be receptive to your professional guidance.

Facilitating peer observations and creating mentor opportunities is a way of being *strategic with delegating* instructional leadership.

Highlighting specific values in dialogue with teachers represents a way of being *intentional* about the focus of instructional practice.

Being *strategic with delegation* represents an attempt to be *intentional* with how you leverage the expertise in your building, ensuring you maximize the collective impact on the instructional program. Being *strategic with delegation* of administrative or clerical tasks also allows you as the instructional leader to be more *intentional* about getting into classrooms.

Removing barriers from teachers earns enormous respect from your teachers and strengthens your *relationships*.

Building a culture focused on student success helps ensure that a *focus on student learning* is a normal part of the way the school functions.

Similarly, providing a consistent *focus on student learning* reinforces a school *culture* that keeps the best interests of students at the forefront.

Being *intentional* is what ensures your *delegation* is actually *strategic*.

Being *curious* about your people facilitates you building stronger *relationships*.

Being *curious* about the circumstances and environment of your teachers assists in *identifying barriers* that need removing.

Being *curious* about the experiences of your students helps you to keep the faculty *focused on their learning*.

Being *curious* about staff morale provides a starting point for strengthening the *culture*.

There is a reason that CURIOSITY was the focus of the first chapter. While some might argue that *relationships* or *culture* are the foundations on which to build this paradigm of instructional leadership, I believe that curiosity is the virtue that represents the true starting point. It is the quality that provides the context or the basis for even caring about the effectiveness of your leadership and the success of your school.

A Case Study

I asked my former Director of Instruction, Dr. Cristy York, to share one of her experiences as an assistant principal because it represented an exemplary example of instructional leadership. Here is her account:

> *Having spent thirteen years teaching 7th-grade social studies and actively participating in professional development, my instructional philosophy and grading methods underwent significant transformations. When I transitioned to the role of Assistant Principal for Instruction at my former school, I immediately recognized the inconsistency and potential controversy surrounding grading practices. Recognizing the challenge ahead, I adopted a methodical, gradual approach to implement lasting positive changes, supported by the principal and fellow assistant principal.*
>
> *To initiate the process, I conducted weekly meetings with each grade level. However, I held off on addressing grading until later in the first year, ensuring teachers were settled and receptive. I started with a survey designed to understand their beliefs about grading, specifically regarding behaviors, effort, participation, late work, extra credit, retakes, homework, zeros, and group work. The survey also questioned the alignment of grading beliefs and practices across the faculty and whether grades truly reflected learning goals. In the first meeting about grading, I shared the survey results, confirming my suspicions: while there were some similarities in beliefs and practices, there were also key areas of misalignment. For instance, most teachers agreed grades were primarily for communication, yet their policies on late work varied dramatically, with some allowing reduced credit, others full credit, and some none at all. This pattern of inconsistency was evident in nearly every grading practice.*

I framed the discussion by focusing on how these inconsistencies might affect students and parents. This led each grade level to the same conclusion: the variance was likely confusing and warranted further exploration. For the remainder of the year, using Ken O'Connor's 15 Fixes for Broken Grades *as a guide, we delved deeper into each area of inconsistency revealed by the survey. I would start each discussion by referencing the survey results to highlight the importance of the topic. Then, I shared O'Connor's insights and proposed solutions. I included real-life examples of how grading practices could negatively impact students and misrepresent their mastery. I also shared my personal experiences with improving grading practices in my own classroom. Finally, teachers had the chance to discuss and brainstorm potential improvements, both individually and as a grade level. For example, when addressing the inclusion of behaviors like effort and participation in grades, I referenced O'Connor's argument that inflated grades distort achievement and his recommendation to report behaviors separately (2011). Teachers then brainstormed which behaviors to report, when to send reports home, and other logistical details. This led to the creation of student self-reflection charts and behavior reports sent to 6th-grade parents. These initiatives were teacher-driven, arising from our discussions, rather than mandated. The first year focused on teacher buy-in, sharing research, facilitating discussions, and allowing teachers to implement changes at their own pace.*

In the second year, teacher interest in grading and assessment as a professional learning topic increased significantly. We reviewed the previous year's work and continued discussing grading beliefs. We then developed a school-wide belief statement: "The purpose of grades is to communicate the degree to which a student has mastered a learning target." We also established a grading platform with three core tenets: grades reflect learning target mastery, students have multiple mastery opportunities, and behavioral feedback is separate from academic grades. This platform helped resolve grading dilemmas. I also shared my struggles, such as giving up grading binder checks, to help lower resistance from teachers. The second year also involved examining complex issues like including formative assessments in grades and aligning assessments with learning targets.

In the third year, we did a faculty-wide book study of John Hattie's 10 Mindframes for Visible Learning, *connecting each mindframe to our established grading platform. This final year focused on refining and reinforcing our platform, grounding it in research-based practices. We ultimately developed a shared understanding of grading, created the grading platform, established two "absolutes"—homework weighted as zero and a minimum report card grade of 50—and identified areas for ongoing improvement.*

So let's consider how the ten strategies were reflected in this process:

Curiosity—This process was predicated on curiosity about the most effective assessment practices. York also spent time surveying teachers about their own attitudes and experiences with grading.

Visibility—York was present and engaged with teachers during this entire process. She also underscored that her principal was present for the collaborative meetings.

Vulnerability—York took a risk leading this process. The faculty could have revolted. They could have resisted any attempt to revise their practices. Moreover, she was vulnerable by sharing her own experiences with grading as a classroom teacher.

Relationships—York's commitment to leading this process in a way that was slow, methodical, and collaborative reflected her commitment to ensuring mutual respect between the administration and the faculty.

Opportunities—York created opportunities for the staff to reflect on their own assessment practices as well as the opportunity to learn from each other.

Delegating—The principal allowed York, his assistant principal, to lead a process that she was passionate about.

- **Intentionality**—York was intentional about providing professional development that ensured her teachers' assessment philosophies were aligned with their assessment practices.
- **A Focus on Learning**—York facilitated a process that was geared toward ensuring assessments were aligned with goals for student learning and that their academic progress was communicated accurately.
- **Removing Barriers / Providing Resources**—York provided two different books to her teachers and lots of time to collaborate to ensure they had the tools and training they needed to develop sound assessment practices.
- **Culture**—York led a process that strengthened the school's culture by focusing on assessment practices that were best for students, by cultivating collaboration among the faculty, and through ensuring common and high expectations for the practices of teachers.

Joy in the Journey

Of all the interviews that I did in preparing for this book, one stands out to me. Karissa Lang is an accomplished and seasoned principal. But what particularly resonated with me was not her knowledge or expertise; it was her passion and her joy. In her concluding remarks, she said, "Servant leadership is to me the greatest leadership quality I think a person can have." She elaborated:

> It is being a servant to your staff, to your kids, and to the parents. The community is trusting you to do the right thing because you're growing the next crop of people who are going to be leading the community. The parents are also sending you their greatest gifts, and your job is to help mold and cultivate them… You've got to jump in with your heart and soul in everything you are and be with them in the journey. All the other pieces will fall in line… If you're all in, and the people know that you're all in… I feel that is where the magic happens.

Lang's joy and passion were palpable during our conversation. My eyes got wet listening to her talk about her commitment to her staff and her students. You see, strategies, knowledge, leadership activities—they all ring hollow if they are not shared in the context of joy, passion, positive energy, and with an authentic commitment to making a difference for your students and staff. Pursuing what Elmore described as the "holy grail" for school leaders is not a very rewarding endeavor if you are not leading from the heart. You have reached this point in your reading, so I suspect you do care and I assume your dedication is intact. The job of a school leader is challenging and stressful, but your work truly matters. Do not be surprised with the bumps in the road, and give yourself grace as you navigate the challenges. Instructional leadership is not something you do to your faculty; it is a way of leading that embraces strategic commitments that are within reach of every school leader. Your experience level, your knowledge base, your context—these may all vary. Your unique dynamics may affect your learning curve, but they don't have to affect your ability to make a positive difference for your teachers and your students. Regardless of your starting point, you can be an instructional leader that moves the needle with student learning. Thank you for embracing the journey. You've got this!

For Product Safety Concerns and Information please contact our EU representative GPSR@taylorandfrancis.com
Taylor & Francis Verlag GmbH, Kaufingerstraße 24, 80331 München, Germany

www.ingramcontent.com/pod-product-compliance
Lightning Source LLC
Chambersburg PA
CBHW070737230426
43669CB00014B/2487